Marc Bolan

ongs, photos, lyrics, interviews, memorabilia,
etters, notes, snapshots, memories...a tribute.

Y0-BRA-785

Wise Publications

Two weeks before his thirtieth birthday, Marc Bolan died in a tragic accident. The car, in which the Rock idol was a passenger, was travelling along a narrow road in South London in the early hours of the morning, when it traversed a hump-backed railway bridge, left the road and crashed into a tree. He was killed instantly.

The national newspapers carried the news of the fatal accident in front-page headlines and momentarily, the popular music world was stunned. Fans, in their hundreds, mourned the loss of their idol, almost turning his funeral into a circus, and to this day, regular visits are made to the scene of the accident, so that sincere and endearingly naive messages can be left, scratched on the tree.

It could be argued that Marc Bolan's death followed the pattern of so many of his peers and an observer of the ephemeral world of Rock 'n' Roll, with all its excesses and extremes, might be forgiven for concluding that a prerequisite to stardom is that the aspirant be prepared to die a violent death, before the age of thirty and at the peak of his career. In his introduction, Steve Turner discusses this very phenomenon.

Because of personal problems, Marc Bolan's career had been on the wane, but at the time of his death, he was on the brink of a certain return to stardom. But he was no run-of-the-mill Rock musician whose greatest attribute is, perhaps, the size of his ego. Marc Bolan was conceited. He was, at times, vain. He was an extraordinarily good looking man, as the numerous photographs of him herein testify. He did have the knack of holding an audience of thousands quietly spellbound, or again, exciting them *en masse* to fever pitch. He did have the facility to write songs that shot into the top of the charts. But on examination, however, it soon becomes apparent that his gifts were rarer than most and of a far deeper quality than many more.

For those who knew him, his charm is unforgettable, and it is these people — his friends, relatives, critics, employees and fellow musicians — who, in their own words and without flattery, tell the story of Marc Bolan.

Ted Dicks

They started to work together and that
was when it became T. Rex—Mickey
and Marc.
They were very beautiful. All the
photographers got off on the visual sort
of thing.

June Bolan

MARC BOLAN
A TRIBUTE

In the production of this book we should like to
acknowledge the assistance of:
Eric Hall, June Bolan, Mick O'Halloran, Adrian the fan,
Paul Jones, Mickey Finn, Robin Nash, Pat Skilton, Elton John,
Alvin Stardust, Mr and Mrs Feld, Jack Steven, B.P. Fallon,
Ros Davies, Geoff Goode, Bob Ireland.

For permission to publish specific news items,
we acknowledge the following publications:
*Daily Mail, Daily Express, The Guardian, Daily Mirror,
Beat Instrumental, Evening Standard, Evening News,
Evening Times, The Sun, Record Mirror.*

For supplying photographic material, we acknowledge the following:
Adrian Boot, Geoff Hildreth, Kevin Cummins, Paul Platz,
Bronwen Hicks, Paul Jones, Steve Finney, Mary Bullen, EMI,
The Rocket Record Company, Magnet Records, Cube Records.

Photograph for back cover by Visconti/Starr.

The quotation from *The Savage God* by A. Alvarez is by kind
permission of the publishers, Weidenfeld & Nicolson.

The Marc Bolan November 1972 interview with Stevie Dixon is by kind
permission of the British Forces Broadcasting Service (London).

Interview with June Bolan, B.P. Fallon, Tony Visconti, Steve Currie,
Jennifer Sharp, Steve Harley, and Gloria Jones, conducted by Stevie Dixon.

Musical illustrations processed by Peter O'Dell and Musicprint.

Cover design by Pearce Marchbank Studio.
Cover photographs by Rex Features.
Research and administration by Paul Platz and Stevie Dixon.
Compiled and edited by Ted Dicks ARCA and Paul Platz.
Concept and design by Ted Dicks ARCA.

Exclusive Distributors:
Music Sales Limited
8/9 Frith Street,
London W1V 5TZ, England.
Music Sales Corporation
257 Park Avenue South
New York, NY10010
United States Of America.
Music Sales Pty Limited
120 Rothschild Avenue,
Rosebery, NSW 2018,
Australia.

This book © Copyright 1992 by Wise Publications
Order No.AM89180
ISBN 0-7119-2995-5

Music Sales' complete catalogue lists thousands of titles and
is free from your local music shop, or direct from Music Sales Limited.
Please send a cheque/postal order for £1.50 for postage to:
Music Sales Limited, Newmarket Road, Bury St. Edmunds, Suffolk IP33 3YB.

Printed in the United Kingdom by
Redwood Books Limited, Trowbridge, Wiltshire.

This book is dedicated to Rolan

CONTENTS

INTRODUCTION

Only of a Rock singer, it seems, could it be said of his violent death at the age of twenty-nine: "Oh, he would have liked it that way."

Marc Bolan, I'm sure, would have seen his car crash death as a suitably stylish means of departure; certainly more in tune with the spirit of Rock than Presley's heart failure at forty-two. They sloganised on the campuses in the sixties: "Never trust anyone over thirty" and Bolan will never have to distrust himself or be distrusted.

In its essence, Rock music and the accompanying culture is about being young. The energy, the vitality, the emotional range, the naivety and the hopes, are youthful. It follows that the greatest sin a Rock 'n' Roller can commit is that of growing old. It is the rank of a traitor; it is stepping over onto the other side. Growing old is giving up; Rock 'n' Roll is a rage against the dying of the light.

A quarter of a century of Rock music has created quite a tradition of dying young, an act often certain of assuring legendary status, even if the preceding life did not warrant it. Legends in their own lifetimes are vaguely boring in Rock, because they just might grow old and spoil everything. One wonders how Cliff Richard, Marty Wilde and Tommy Steele might be regarded today if they had met tragic ends in the early sixties. It is certain that the subsequent years unravelled their hard Rock 'n' Roll reputations as they drifted into more middle-of-the-road entertainment.

Those that die young are eternal adolescents who never grow older and more comfortable. They can be trusted.

Buddy Holly died at the age of twenty-two in a plane crash, along with seventeen-year-old Ritchie Valens and the twenty-six-year-old Big Bopper.

Eddie Cochran, author of SUMMERTIME BLUES, died in a car crash at twenty-one; Gene Vincent of a stomach ulcer at thirty-six.

Who is to say what kind of music any of them would be producing today? Buddy Holly would be forty years old, Cochran thirty-nine. Gene Vincent was on the downward slide when he died anyway, but the death served to revive new interest.

At the end of the sixties came another rash of deaths after a relatively calm period during the Beatles reign. It began with Rolling Stone Brian Jones, and continued with Jimi Hendrix, Janis Joplin and Jim Morrison. Since then, two members of the Allman Brothers Band and members (or ex-members) of the Average White Band, Stone the Crows, The Byrds, Badfinger, Free, The Grateful Dead, The Flying Burrito Brothers, The Yardbirds, The Shadows and Deep Purple, have met with accidental deaths. All in all, some forty-five chart-rated performers have died over the past two decades, the average age being twenty-eight years old.

Accidental deaths by their nature are not planned, although, in many of the cases above, there had been strong suspicions of a death wish, or a deliberately suicidal lifestyle.

In the cases of Rock stars, the wish for death may not simply be through despair or the 'pressures of life at the top' but through something that is more deeply embedded in the Rock consciousness, the fear of growing old, the fear of ageing into a traitor. When your whole life has been based on a premise of youthful excess, each year takes you nearer to hypocrisy. The archetypal life and death for Rock 'n' Roll came right at its birth in 1955 and was that of a man who never sang or played a guitar: James Dean.

Just as his life was regarded as a spit in the eye to any force that might tame his youthful aggressive spirit, so was his death revered as a refusal to enter into the conventional adulthood. The means of his death, a car smash, while speeding along an open Californian road, contained all the elements necessary to preserve the legend; speed, solitude, defiance and an instant cut-off. Most of us are forced to grow older, more responsible, less idealistic, but James Dean showed that even these seemingly most certain of processes could be defeated.

The spirit of James Dean in life and death has pervaded Rock culture. His moodiness, his slouch and his arrogance have been copied by Rock stars from Presley onwards, and the idea of 'burning out like a comet' rather than growing old, is seen as the most desirable way of ending things. As with the Romantic poets, the doomed lifestyle is perfected by Rock artists to the point where it is taken as a compliment to be described as 'wasted'. An American Rock magazine even went so far as to organise a competition to devise a list of Rock stars likely to die next. A. Alvarez, writing of the Romantics, in THE SAVAGE GOD, sums up the mood well:

> "In varying degrees ... death was literally, their final Cleopatra. But they conceived of death and suicide childishly: Not as an end of everything but as the supreme, dramatic gesture of contempt towards a dull bourgeois world."

Never has a form of entertainment or art centred itself so securely around reverence for youth. While the 'old' may still go on playing, they tend to take on either museum value, admit their age and 'go comfortable' or become an embarrassing spectacle of mutton posing as lamb.

Marc Bolan was all about style. The photographs show it; the careful attention given to dress, his affection for the camera, his ability to absorb the latest in Rock culture and somehow make it his own. The records show it; poetry for the Hippies, rhythm for the Rockers, and a lashing of pop for the 'teenies'. In his career he touched all bases from Carnaby Street to Tolkien, to Glitter, but he never actually 'sold out' in the pejorative sense of the word. He was always 'sold out' to the spirit of Rock 'n' Roll and whatever was that year's manifestation.

As in life, so in death. Whereas most of the world aims for their life to end in their sleep during their eighties, the stylish Rock 'n' Roll ending has you extinguished just as you burn brightest, while the flame is still hot. One expects Marc would have approved, in principle, the idea of a car crash at the age of twenty-nine being a suitable means of dying. Rock is a religion based on the worship of adolescence; the faithful give their lives rather than become apostate.

Steve Turner

Libra is the 7th sign of the Zodiac, the symbol being an empty scale, which indicates that a Libran is without a life of his own; furthermore, in order to function he would need constant stimulation from others. Venus is the ruling planet for Libra, which accounts for the Libran's sociability and beauty. The typical Libran has natural good looks and is blessed with an easy-going disposition — just as long as he gets his own way. Conversely the sign of Libra can be the most ungrateful of all the Zodiac; it is certainly the vainest, even to the point of narcissism.

The most distinctive features of the typical Libran are the eyes and wide jaw; the eyes are generally large and wide open. When in repose and untroubled, the Libran face is possibly the most beautiful face of the Zodiac.

The body is usually graceful and often athletic. Being vain, the Libran has the constant urge to exhibit the 'body beautiful'. He will tend to use his attractiveness to obtain whatever he needs, but there is also the necessity for others to need and want him.

The Libran is a taker, not a giver, but will often give beautiful presents in order to hide his true intentions. The male is even more vain than the female; thus many politicians are Librans, because of their need to be in the public eye and their liking for applause. But because of the Libran's innate sense of style, he is often successful in the worlds of art, or graphic design, dancing and the theatre.

He is determined to succeed: nevertheless he has no pride in admitting failure and starting anew.

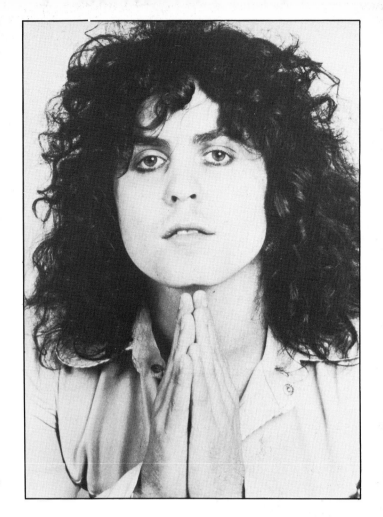

THE STRONG LIBRAN

FOUR PLANETS IN LIBRA

During the production of this book, a professional astrologer was approached with the intention that a chart be cast and drawn on Marc Bolan's life. The astrologer was given Marc Bolan's hour and date of birth, and sex, but his identity was withheld.

The chart duly cast and drawn, the astrologer was then asked to account the characteristics, talents, influences and potential attributes of her anonymous subject as revealed astrologically. The result was an uncanny parallel to what we know as being actual fact and is yet further testimony to those special qualities bestowed upon Marc Bolan.

One further point; the astrologer was not told that her subject had died, thus, sadly, she speaks of him in the present tense.

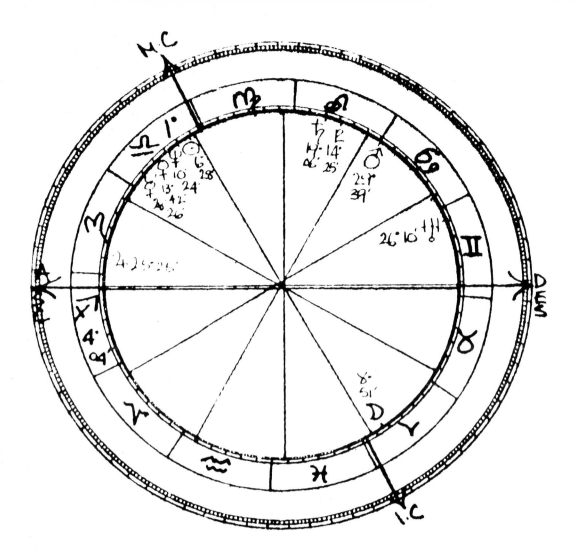

The subject is very strong Libran. This is because he has four planets in Libra. He also has Sagittarius rising, which means he is restless; always shooting arrows that do not all necessarily come to ground. He is always striving and searching for the bigger and the better and he has, in consequence, big plans and big ideas. He is someone, in fact, of whom it can be said is large in concept.

But let me first speak about his physical characteristics. It is very apparent that he is physically attractive and has a face that can best be described as charming, a face that is always likely to break into a smile. He is dark, well built but small; everything, however, is put together in the right place. There is nothing physically big about the subject, nothing out of place, nothing unbalanced. In short, he is beautifully proportioned.

The chart is intensely spiritual. In fact, one could say that spiritual is the key word. He is passionately involved with 'other-worldliness', almost to the point where it is difficult for the subject to keep his feet on the ground. He is in another dimension, as it were. He has a total involvement in other concepts, such as para-psychology, the spiritual, the metaphysical, magic — all that sort of thing. This spiritual aspect is very strong indeed, probably to the point of weakness, in that the subject would rather not face up to hard reality. There would be a tendency to drugs perhaps, or

drink maybe; some form of escape. There would be a tendency to fantasise, having a loose grip on what is actually going on. At the same time though, let me quickly add an almost contradictory factor; there is this great striving for success and achievement. The whole chart is geared to making this urge almost all-consuming. It is essential for him to produce something that is not only tangible and real, but beautiful. And this in itself is difficult for him; to have the need to produce something concrete but, at the same time, to have to constantly fight to grasp the cold sober reality of anything. I'll go as far as to say that this discord within himself could lead to psychological problems.

There is a further dichotomy in his make-up, where one basic characteristic is in direct conflict with another. Librans always need other people; they can hardly ever survive on their own. You might say that a Libran is half a person and thus needs a soul-mate. But at the same time, this subject, at times, urgently desires to be on his own, by himself; there is this great need for seclusion and isolation before production can be achieved. So strong is this need, that if denied, there is the possibility of the subject losing a sense of reality and causing everything to become merely frivolous. It is as if he needs that isolation — peace, if you will — to recharge himself, to analyse everything around him and bring his world into perspective.

The artistic potential is tremendous. It is as if his whole life is there for one purpose and one purpose only: artistic achievement. Very little else would matter to him really. Not a day goes by without this desire to create something, visual, verbal, whatever. There seems to be a potential to do anything and everything on an artistic level. But it should be pointed out that there is an acid streak here, certainly in the spoken word; there is this cutting edge to his talent, this sharpness. Again, we have a paradox. His chart shows a general sweetness of tone, angelic, if you wish, but there is also this strong indication of a tendency to cut with words; sarcastic and quick to anger.

It is a very sharp mind, intelligent and extremely original. He is always wanting — needing — to think of something new and is never satisfied. The chart is totally Air orientated, Air representing the mind, so it follows he has this need to think and to be free to think. There is a constant flow of ideas there and were the subject forced to be constricted by doing something humdrum, repetitive, he would be extremely unhappy. He is easily bored and thus, always wanting change.

There is, however, a marked selfish, egotistical streak pervading through his chart. There is heat and strength which is in direct antagonism with the soft part of his nature. Another conflict; another dichotomy. It is almost as if there is a man and a woman in his nature, fighting for supremacy, the male part being very concerned with self and with what the self can do, to the exclusion of what other people might want. A terrible conflict this, but nevertheless, it is the very thing that makes the subject as productive and creative as he is. The femininity in his chart — of which I would like to say more later — is that which makes him so artistic and, in turn, being so strong an aspect of his make-up, it is this that would make him something of an exhibitionist.

Relationships with women are extremely emotional. There is a constant need to be in love. And to be loved. As I have said, there is a very strong female aspect in his chart and this would indicate a tendency to bi-sexuality. There is, also, a need to feel like a woman feels and to be allowed that expression. Because the emotional drive is basically an intuitive, soft, incoming thing, rather than an aggressive thing — in spite of the verbal aggression I mentioned earlier — the emotional feeling he experiences is totally subjective and all-absorbing.

Finally, the subject is very accident prone. I should suspect that, from an early age, being a hasty person, always rushing into things, always wanting the quick solution to anything, there will be times when there would be accidents; cuts, burns, falls, this sort of thing. Let us say that accidents are likely and the most likely area to be affected would be the head.

At this point, the astrologer was told that her subject was, in fact, dead; given this information, she concluded thus:

I should suspect that death was a sudden release; no suffering as with a prolonged illness, but his departure would most likely have been instantaneous.

Reina James.

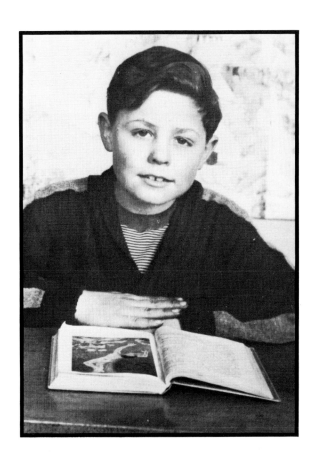

. . . Our lives are merely trees of possibilities. . . .

DE 543172			CERTIFIED COPY of an ENTRY OF BIRTH. Pursuant to the Births and Deaths Registration Acts, 1836 to 1929.					[Printed by Authority of the Registrar-General.] B. Cert. R.B.D.	

The Statutory Fee for this Certificate is 2s. 6d. together with 1d. Stamp Duty. Where a search is necessary to find the entry, a Search Fee is payable in addition.

Insert in this Margin any Notes which appear in the original entry.

	Registration District					HACKNEY			
1947	Birth in the Sub-District of					in the			

Columns:	1	2	3	4	5	6	7	8	9	10
No.	When and Where Born.	Name, if any.	Sex.	Name and Surname of Father.	Name and Maiden Surname of Mother.	Rank or Profession of Father.	Signature, Description and Residence of Informant.	When Registered.	Signature of Registrar.	Baptismal Name, if added after Registration of Birth.
173	Thirtieth September 1947 Hackney Hospital	Mark	Boy	Simeon Feld	Phyllis Winifred Feld formerly Atkins	Cosmetic Salesman 123 Stoke Newington Common Stoke Newington	P. W. Feld mother 23 Stoke Newington Common n.16.	First October 1947	G. Weaver Deputy Registrar.	

I, GLADYS WEAVER Deputy Registrar of Births and Deaths for the Sub-District of HACKNEY SOUTH EAST , in the do hereby certify that this is a true copy of the Entry No. 173 in the Register Book of Births for the said Sub-District, and that such Register Book is now legally in my custody

WITNESS MY HAND this 1st day of October 1947.

G. Weaver Deputy
Registrar of Births and Deaths.

CAUTION.—Any person who (1) falsifies any of the particulars on this Certificate, or (2) uses it as true, knowing it to be falsified, is liable to Prosecution.

MARC BOLAN

HIS STORY

AS TOLD BY THOSE

WHO KNEW HIM

He was born at Hackney Hospital, East London, on September 30th 1947, the second son of Phyllis and Syd Feld, and christened Mark.

I danced myself out of the womb
Is it strange to dance so soon
I danced myself into the tomb
But then again once more
I danced myself out of the womb
Is it strange to dance so soon
I danced myself out of the womb.
From COSMIC DANCER by Marc Bolan

The family lived in a terraced house in Stoke Newington, London. His father was a cosmetic salesman, augmenting his income at weekends by running a stall in Petticoat Lane, selling junk jewellery. His mother ran a fruit stall in Berwick Street Market, in the Soho district of London.

His first school was Northwood Primary, and it was at this time, it is said, that he became close friends with Keith Reid, later of Procol Harum fame.

On occasions he would help his mother at her fruit stall and because of its close proximity to the Two I's coffee bar (around the corner in Old Compton Street and where such talents as Tommy Steele and Cliff Richard were first discovered) it is said that he would often visit and help serve coffee. He later admitted that he himself auditioned there but was turned down.

I was dancing when I was eight
Is it strange to dance so late
I danced myself into the tomb
Is it strange to dance so soon
I danced myself into the tomb.
From COSMIC DANCER by Marc Bolan

At the age of eleven he went to the William Wordsworth Secondary School. He joined his first pop group, Susie and the Hula Hoops, the group's singer being Helen Shapiro, who was to achieve international acclaim as the schoolgirl singing star.

I was dancing when I was twelve
I was dancing when I was aaah
I danced myself right out of the womb
Is it strange to dance so soon
I danced myself right out of the womb.
From COSMIC DANCER by Marc Bolan

When he was fourteen, the family moved to South London and he went to Hill Croft School. But not for long.

Marc Bolan, Nov. 1972:
I left school at fourteen. I was expelled. It was all very amiable. I just didn't think they were teaching me the things I wanted to know. I only had about six months to go anyway. I just didn't go anymore. No one seemed to mind very much. So it was nice.

He began to show a marked interest in poetry and romantic literature, chief among the many writers to influence him being Dylan Thomas and Rimbaud.

Is it wrong to understand
The fear that dwells inside a man
What's it like to be a loon
I liken it to a balloon.
From COSMIC DANCER by Marc Bolan

Eric Hall:
Creative Manager, ATV music, and close friend of Marc Bolan
There used to be a place, a 'schtip' house, like an amusement place with pinball machines and that sort of thing; 'schtip' in Jewish means like to take money from someone. Well, every Stamford Hill boy used to meet at this 'schtip' house. I'd be about twelve. I, or my brothers, would buy magazines like *Vogue* or *Town*, and you'd see a picture of this young boy model; very smart good-looking boy; the local boy made good: Mark Feld. Even in those days he was a star. I was about fifteen when I first actually met him. He'd be about fourteen, I guess. He was still at school and modelling in his spare time; not officially, of course. But he always knew a million people. Used to go to clubs. If I remember right, it was the El Toro club in St John's Wood, or maybe it was Finchley Road. It was a sort of local Jewish type disco. Mind you, most of the guys were in their early twenties, like five years older than Marc. It was mainly a gay situation. They got to like Marc of course, and used to get him the odd job on magazines.

Marc Bolan age six

He played a small part in a TV series as a delinquent opposite the actor Sam Kydd. He modelled suits for the tailoring chain, John Temple. He served in a clothing shop in Tooting, meanwhile washing dishes in a Wimpy Bar in the evenings.
With the American actor, Riggs O'Hara, he went to Paris, where, it is said, he studied magic with a middle-aged man whom he later referred to as 'the Wizard'.

He failed his first recording test with EMI, but with Decca he made his first single with a song entitled THE WIZARD, the B side being BEYOND THE RISING SUN. The label bore the name of Marc Bowland, Decca promoters apparently deciding that the name of Mark Feld was not sufficiently outstanding. For a while, however, he adopted the alias of Toby Tyler, folk singer. His first manager was Simon Napier Bell and through him he became a member of the pop group, John's Children, remembered chiefly for their advertising campaign featuring posters throughout London showing the group in the nude. The group toured Germany with The Who, and for the group he wrote DESDEMONA.

Occasionally, he found it necessary to busk in the streets.

Drawing by Marc aged fourteen

Marc Bolan, Nov. 1972:
I used to make about £30 a day, but you have to work really hard from, like nine in the morning to midnight. And after a while you lose your voice. And it's cold.

> O the throat of winter is upon us
> The barren barley fields refuse to sway
> Before the husky hag of early darkness
> In her hoods of snowy grey.
> Winter Winter Winter
> Are you but a servant of the bad one.
>
> Lo the frozen blue birds in the belfries
> The bluebells in their hearts are surely prey
> Unto the grasping bats-wing of the winter pincer
> Hoods of snowy grey.
> THE THROAT OF WINTER by Marc Bolan

A lot of 'hype' went down and I did *Ready Steady Go* and all those sort of things.

B. P. Fallon:
Publicist for Marc Bolan and close friend
I first sort of met him at *Ready Steady Go* which would be about 1966. He was on with Jimi Hendrix. It was an amazing show really, because there were these two — to use a cliché — these two magical people on it and they were heavily vibe-ing each other. I was fascinated by him, but, at that time, it was a sort of faraway fascination.

Marc Bolan, Nov. 1972:
Not much happened, though there was quite a lot of interest in me at the time. But I was bored with doing it that way, so I spent two years really mastering the art of songwriting and playing the guitar as much as I could.

June Bolan:
née Childs; wife to Marc Bolan and guiding administrator to T. Rex
I first met Marc in 1967. I was working for Blackhill Enterprises, that little office in Alexander Street. Marc came in to see Pete Jenner and Andrew King. He wanted us to manage him; we had The Floyd, you see, and Marc loved Syd Barrett. I was in my office, but I kept feeling this banging on my head; it was a most extraordinary feeling. I went in and asked them if they wanted coffee, that's all. And then off he went, looking very odd. He had his mother's trousers on, a pair of flying boots and a school blazer full of holes. "What a funny looking little thing!" I thought, but with eyes you just could not believe.

It was a physical thing; as I said, like someone had hit me over the head. But that was Marc. He could walk into a room looking like death from the back of beyond, a right little scruff arse! But he still had that charismatic thing. I mean, it wasn't as if he was famous then; it wasn't as if I was attracted by his reputation or anything.... Anyway, Pete and Andrew asked me what I thought of him. I said that I'd heard *Perfumed Garden*, the show John Peel was doing on the radio, and I said I liked it; I'd only heard two songs which he had done on the show but it was so different, something just had to happen....

Marc Bolan aged fourteen

... and you'd see a picture of this young boy model; very smart good-looking boy; the local boy made good: Mark Feld.

John Peel:
BBC Radio One Disc Jockey
I first heard from Marc when I was working on Radio London, the pirate station in 1967. I had just come back from California. This was after he'd left John's Children and he sent me an acetate and some tapes of songs that he'd recorded on his own or with Steve Took. He asked me what I thought of them. I liked them very well and because of the way you could do that sort of thing on Radio London, I played the acetates on the air.

June Bolan:
... Next day they had a gig at Ealing College and Andrew suggested we go along and see what they were like live,

Marc and June in their cold-water flat

Steve Took and Marc Bolan

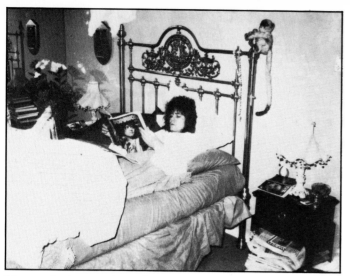

Marc relaxing and reading a pop magazine, the cover of which is a portrait of himself.

Marc and Steve Took. It was a lunch session and we arrived about half way through and watched till the end. They had a little Vox AC amplifier, no PA, no nothing, just a microphone and a bent coat-hanger. But he had that something you can't deny. Afterwards we said we'd drive them back. Incidentally, The Floyd had a Bentley and as I was the only one insured to drive it, I drove. For me, in those days, that was a big deal. I was only twenty and as far as I was concerned, only posh people drove around in Bentleys. Anyway, we took Marc back to his mother's house; she had a little prefab in Wimbledon called 'Summertime', so we dropped them there and I went back to work with Andrew. About an hour later the telephone rang. It was Marc. He said he had to see me immediately and I thought, "Oh my God, problems already!" I told Andrew and Pete and, thinking it was business, they said I'd better go over. When I got there I went in and Marc said: "I'm in love with you and I don't know what to do about it." ... and it was just wonderful.

> All my days are leafy blue
> Because I'm not with you
> All my words are ragged steel
> When I'm not with you,
> See how the sun shines
> Like an arc where you walk
> All my fears are water clear
> When I'm not with you
> All I hear is wicked dear
> When I'm not with you.   DOVE by Marc Bolan

John Peel:
... I liked him as a human being and I liked his music. From that time on, whenever I had a gig anywhere, I would ask Marc and Steve to go along and play. Often the people who were running the gig were not terribly pleased about it, because they didn't like people sitting on the stage banging children's instruments and singing in a bizarre manner. Eventually people started to like it and we did a lot of gigs together; I suppose about twenty, twenty-five, something like that.

June Bolan:
He was getting about £5 a gig. Because he lived out at Wimbledon, the taxi home, with all his 'bits and bobs', cost him about £5!

John Peel:
I was billed over them but then the billing started to change. They were Tyrannosaurus Rex introduced by John Peel, which, of course, is the way it should have been. From then on, obviously things just started to get better and better from Marc's point of view.

In concert, the John Peel Show, 1968

June Bolan:
Two days after we met, we decided we'd live together. I had a Hillman Commer; I was very proud of it, I remember. It cost me £40 and I had a mattress in the back. I just had to be with him, so I went over to his mother's house, knocked on the door, picked him up and we spent the next four nights on Wimbledon Common in my little van.

Danae Brook, *Evening News*, March 10th 1978:
In those days Marc and Steve Took used to play free in the park. Marc with his acoustic guitar and voice, Steve with his bongo drums and harmonies.

June Bolan, as told to Danae Brook, *Evening News*:
They used to sit in the grass and people would gather round to listen. Freebies. That's how gigs were then.

Danae Brook, *Evening News*:
Before long Marc had moved out of the park and into the Middle Earth in Covent Garden. It was a place where kids could listen and dance to live music.

Tony Visconti:
Record producer; a major contributor to Marc Bolan's success
I was told by both my bosses, David Platz and Denny Cordell, to go out and find a group to produce. I went around a few clubs; at that time—this would be in 1967— there were just Rock groups, flower power groups. One night I went into the UFO club and saw Tyrannosaurus

Rex on stage with a group of about three hundred mesmerised people around. There was a very bad PA system but the thing that cut through was Marc's very, very unusual voice, he was very warbly in those days. Also, I noticed the audience reaction; it was more than music they were reacting to; they were mesmerised by his image.

June Bolan:

I mean, he could only play four chords or something. But he'd sit down in the middle of the room, cross-legged, with an acoustic guitar, and sing songs that people had never heard. They didn't even have words that rhymed; they weren't moon and June songs. They had odd words, odd sentences full of weird mythological references, half his own and half he'd picked up from Greek and Persian mythology; things he would churn around and bring out Bolan.

> The wind quartet howls softly
> My jeep hand strokes her necklace
> Crusted, crammed with old Etruscan gold.
>
> Her bird head torn with summer
> Inspects a Spartan runner
> Robbing time a chosen Prince of Speed
>
> My goblet drenched with Autumn
> Tears for my dead cat Ena
> Silver Surfer sorcerer of spray
>
> She hooded deep in chartreuse
> A falcon glimpse of white teeth
> Separated by lace cinnamon folds
>
> We hid and rid in Hansom
> Cab wrenched from lost Byzantium
> Lordlett who once held the earth in chains.
>   WIND QUARTETS by Marc Bolan

... He had an extraordinary mind for somebody totally self-educated.

June
the focus of my eyes, that for one full rich year has gazed deeply in the crystal panes of the window of your soul, have been bruised by the planets & they have blured my foolish vision with all my young being I desired that, that blessed focus should once more look long & true into the wooded regions of your mind & body

rember I have & do

love you

your, for ever as I am & with the gods grace shall remain

your

Marc

A letter to June.

Marc Bolan, Nov. 1972:
I don't really read too much in what people say. I suppose to the average Rock 'n' Roller I might be considered slightly eccentric or out of the ordinary for them. I did study magic when I was about sixteen and I learnt a lot about the other things that go in the universe, but I always knew those things anyway. I just didn't know if they were true or not. In my early writings, I wrote about . . . well, I used the science fiction media to express myself because at that time, that was the feeling that was going around.

Tony Visconti:
On such a low budget, he was dressed in rags and he was playing a twelve-quid guitar. . . .

June Bolan:
He had a little guitar, a Sazooki Gibson copy, one of those Japanese copies. I used to take it to the hock shop on the Friday and hock it when the rent was due. By luck something would always turn up that would give us the money by the Monday, so we could go and get the guitar back.

Tony Visconti:
. . . The drummer was playing on borrowed drums, Steve Peregrine Took. I was amazed by all this and said that I must produce this act. To me, a group isn't worth doing unless they're slightly different and in this case, they were radically different; I got myself a handful.
Marc was so weird and strange-looking and his singing was so odd; he really did look like the 'bopping elf'. I was afraid to approach him. I went up to the drummer instead, but he referred me straight back to Marc. Marc was sort of full of himself that night. He was having a very successful gig and he said: "You're about the sixth record producer who came up to me this week. I'll consider you. What did you say your name was?" Then he said: "John Lennon's asked to produce me, you know." He was making it all up of course. He always tended to . . . exaggerate.

June Bolan:
He had an extraordinary mind for somebody totally self-educated. I mean, he did go to school but he loathed everything about it. To him it was a complete waste.

Tony Visconti:
I think I must have been the only record producer who approached him in ages, because he was in my office the very next day. He and Steve Took came up and played for Denny Cordell in the office, they auditioned for him right then and there. They were very weird but Denny knew about the flower thing, so he said: "There'll be underground things happening so we'll call them our token underground group." With that, he gave me a budget of about—oh, I don't know—about £400. That was virtually four days in the studio. We made that first album, including the single DEBORA; it was recorded, over-dubbed and mixed in four days. That was the very beginning.

Danae Brook, *Evening News*:
"It was fun to be alive," June remembers. "There were new sounds, new painters, new philosophies."
Marc's sensitive lyrics spoke to a whole generation of growing young people. He was part of the changes they were going through and his music reflected both the vision and realities.

> At the birth of the day
> As a babe of the spray
> Like a white star
> Tangled and far
> Tulip that's what you are.
>
> Warm and wise as a mute
> In the thunderbolt suit
> Princely and torn
> Grasping the horn
> Of the maenads of May.
>
> Sleepy dreaming of dark
> Silver Satyrs in parks
> Statues that say
> Worship the day
> For only humans you are.
>
> Channels churning the grime
> Inky dreams of our time
> Into the Sun
> Where the white one
> Poems them into a rhyme.
>
> On a hill the clear shrill
> Made the Titans most ill
> Angels abound
> And I kissing the ground
> Thrilled to be around.
>
> Vineyards spangled with love
> For the white dove above
> Green and lean from the waste
> Of the pastures of chaste
> Preciously he is whole.
>
> Tinkled eyes like a king
> Chartered spas on your skin
> Like a white star
> Tangled and far
> Tulip that's what you are.
>   LIKE A WHITE STAR by Marc Bolan

June Bolan:
We didn't have anywhere to live so we found a cold-water attic in a house in Blenheim Crescent. It cost three pounds eight and sixpence a week; no bathroom, not even in the whole house. We lived there for three years. I worked for Blackhill for a year and Marc wrote songs, played music and did the odd gig.

Tony Visconti:
He was very adaptable. On his low budget he was able to make the whole Tyrannosaurus Rex thing happen. They started it at the Roundhouse gig. They were making five quid a night and then within two months of completing

Tony Visconti and Marc Bolan.

the album, after it was out, they were up to — like — sixty quid a night and then a hundred and twenty quid a night, very rapidly.

Mick O'Halloran:
Marc Bolan's roadie until Aug. 1977
It was about 1969 when I first started working for Marc and I remember quite clearly how I got the job. I used to work for a pop group called Love Affair; they had several hits but at the time they were cutting down on all expenses, so me and another chap, called Charlie, were given our notice. At the time we used to buy all our equipment from a company at Kennington Oval and one of the persons there that we got reasonably friendly with was a woman called Pinky. She knew I was married and got a child so she said : "I know a really smashing job that would suit you ; working for Tyrannosaurus Rex." At that time I'd never even heard of them.

June Bolan:
Gradually the gigs got a bit more ; I mean, twenty pounds a night — I mean, twenty pounds ! That was a fortune. We used to have to pay our rent monthly. It was twenty-eight pounds, nine and sixpence and to find twenty-eight pounds, nine and six in one go was almost impossible.

Tony Visconti:
He could always deal with success on any level ; he was always taking advantage of it, always taking the next step. He quit Peter Jenner and Andrew King (Blackhill Enterprises) because they were still accepting gigs at twenty-

five quid. Marc knew he could get more. One day he pulled the phone right out of Peter Jenner's hand and said : "No. Tyrannosaurus Rex go up for a hundred quid a night now." He left Peter Jenner and Andrew King and took their secretary with him, June, and she became his roadie. I mean, he knew how to use people and he knew what he wanted. As I say, he could cope on any level of success.

B. P. Fallon:
I met Marc again in '69 at Island Records. He'd come round to see Chris Blackwell, to look for management. Chris had referred him to some people called EG Management ; I was the Island press officer at the time. Strangely, what happened was I found I was doing a lot of work at Island for King Crimson, who had just started, and I went and joined Crimson's management, who had Marc — EG Management.

Mick O'Halloran:
I got in touch with somebody called Jean who suggested I go along after two o'clock for an interview. I turned up there, knocked at the door and someone looked out of the window at the top flat and shouted : "Won't be a minute. I'll come down and let you in." So I waited for a few minutes and suddenly the door opened and who should appear was this little person, beautiful looking, with really curly hair ! Most unbelievable person I've ever seen at that period of time. I couldn't believe my eyes, you know ?

Tony Visconti:
As early as '71 or '72 he called himself a Cosmic Punk.

June Bolan, as told to Danae Brook, *Evening News*:
He was the first person to coin that phrase here. He used to say in interviews: "I'm just a punk. An East End punk." He was completely self-taught but he read a lot, and I think he picked it up as an American slang word from the twenties, when he was reading Steinbeck.

B. P. Fallon:
He was a teaser. He liked to gently say "fuck you" to people.

Eric Hall:
I don't know of anybody who didn't like him.

Mick O'Halloran:
I said: "I've come about the job."
He said: "Oh. Come in. I thought you were the taxi-driver."
So I said: "No. I've come about the job as a roadie."
We got talking and he gave me a cup of coffee. And in talking to him I realised it was Marc Bolan.

... What happened was that I slowly began to cut the words down. Most poets do, you'll find. ...

June Bolan:
I lived my life through him and although I was much better educated than him, and much more worldly in an everyday sense, if you know what I mean — I mean, I used to do all the business deals and the tax schemes and this, that and the other, because he didn't have one practical iota in his body. But he was my total creative outlook. I used to spend hours listening to him play, watching him write, typing all his words.

Marc Bolan, Nov. 1972:
What happened was that I slowly began to cut the words down. Most poets do, you'll find. After a couple of years of writing flowery poetry — and I don't down that, but it's not really suited to Rock 'n' Roll particularly — things I write now are just street poems. I do write stories which are probably like the old songs really, but I wanted to reach as many people as possible and I was beginning to think that wasn't the way to do it.

> Torch girl of the marshes
> Her kiss is a whip of the moon
> Dawn's damsels are dancing
> To the hum of her sunny young tune
> Ho ho, elemental child
> Ho ho, yeah yeah,
> Elemental child
> Elemental child
> Hold the glove of gold behind you
> Love the glove of Truth.
>
> Gems hemmed in her heart's head
> The shield of the rivers is hers
> She once told me to think white
> And the night disappeared like a bird
> Ho ho, elemental child
> Ho ho, yeah yeah
> Elemental child
> Elemental child
> Hold the glove of gold behind you
> Love the glove of Truth.
>
> ELEMENTAL CHILD by Marc Bolan

Toni Visconti:
June could talk to him. She could get through to him.

Danae Brook, *Evening News*:
She is independent, energetic and practically creative. It was her dynamism coupled to Marc's musicianship and ability to write which enabled him to achieve the thing he most wanted — stardom.
But it was stardom that eventually destroyed his emotional security, his creative output, his physical appearance and, perhaps, finally his life.

B. P. Fallon:
It was an amazing adventure, first of all.

Mick O'Halloran:
Everywhere we seemed to go luck just seemed to follow us.

B. P. Fallon:
There was a gig in Nottingham. And it broke. That's when the Rock 'n' Roll tide turned and Boley started becoming a Rock 'n' Roll icon. We talked about it after the gig. It was an inexplicable feeling.

Mick O'Halloran:
They would sit and listen to him, even just to talk; he used to talk to them. I don't know whether he hypnotised them or what, but he used to sit down on the floor, cross-legged, and be able to hold an audience for a good ten minutes, maybe even more, without even playing a note. From the time he used to walk on the stage, very casual, he used to relax people.

B. P. Fallon:
You must remember he'd always been strong on the stage before he had hit records. He'd always drawn large audiences. . . . He exuded an incredible timelessness.

Mick O'Halloran:
The thing about Marc was that he loved everybody; he just loved people in general.

Marc Bolan, as told to David Neill, *Record Weekly:*
If you take time to talk to any cats, you find they are basically nice. But people don't take the trouble to find out.

B. P. Fallon:
It's very weird going to *Top of the Pops* first time. You know, the smaller you were, the earlier you had to be there. We went along and they were really surprised we all weren't — like — tripping and falling all over the place, sort of wafting around. They wouldn't let us in to the BBC bar; we were sitting on the floor outside, waiting for the magical permission to go into this sacred place, the bloody BBC bar. Boley said: "What do they expect us to do? Drink dewdrops out of rose petals?"

June Bolan:
The first time we went to America (Marc, Steve and I) their agent and booker was a guy called Steve O'Rourke, at present Pink Floyd's manager. Steve Took was very heavy into acid, but very heavy; not just an indulger but he was taking two or three trips a day. He became just like a vegetable and on stage — a stage about as big as you'd get in a tiny club that seated about a hundred people — he would suddenly start taking his clothes off and beating himself with belts and things like that. This was like ten years ago. It was ridiculous. When you've only got two people on stage, a guitar player and a bongo player, you can't have the bongo player not playing bongo and you're just left with an acoustic guitar. There was no electric guitar then. We left Steve in America; we abandoned him. He met this chick and said he didn't think he was coming back, so we just said for him to go. We came back to England, not knowing what we were going to do.

Mick O'Halloran:
They'd played a few underground clubs in New York which I believe were very successful, at that time, but they didn't go back. They stayed away for some reason. I believe Marc was waiting for a hit record before he would attempt it again. He'd seen what the States was like and I think that's what he was waiting for — a hit record.

June Bolan:
One day we were in this pub — I think it was the Roebuck, King's Road, and somebody said — for the life of me I can't think who — but somebody said they'd got a friend who decorates houses and plays good bongos. It was Mickey Finn, who looked so extraordinary; he was so good looking, really beautiful. Marc needed sombody who could sing because Steve Took did good harmonies and good backing vocals. Mickey couldn't sing a bloody note, but he looked so splendid and played reasonable bongos.

Mickey Finn and Marc Bolan.

Mick O'Halloran:
They introduced me to a guy named Mickey. Me, being a bit naive, didn't really know anything about the underground pop scene. They explained a little bit about it: "There's only two in the band and Mickey plays percussion; just a few bongo drums, and bells and things."

June Bolan:
They started to work together and that was when it became T. Rex — Mickey and Marc.
They were very beautiful. All the photographers got off on the visual sort of thing.

Mickey Finn:
Percussionist of T. Rex
It was really good to work with him; it was great. We clicked and played together. It was like — wow!

IMPERIAL COLLEGE CHARITY CARNIVAL

Present a

Folk Concert

in aid of the LEUKEMIA RESEARCH FUND

STARRING

DONOVAN

with

TYRANNOSAURUS REX
THE FLAME

COMPERE **JOHN PEEL**

THURSDAY 21st MARCH

ROYAL ALBERT HALL
Manager F. J. MUNDY

1/-

An early concert programme.

Mick O'Halloran:
They had an album out called BEARD OF STARS which was, in my eyes, a beautiful album. Very sort of cheaply done, but lovely effects on it, and he played most of the things himself.

The Sun, May 18th 1970:
Man with magic in his head.
BEARD OF STARS, latest LP from that imaginative pop duo Tyrannosaurus Rex, contains lore from the books of Agadinmar.
It is dedicated to the Priests of Peace, all Shepherds and

Horse Lords and my Imperial Lore Liege — the King of the Rumbling Spires.
I asked Marc Bolan, long-time half of the TR, who all these historic figures were.
"They're just in my head," he said. "Agadinmar is a name assimilated from the books, a knowledge source. The priests of Peace are a reference to my guardian angel. I'm quite a religious person. The Rumbling Spires comes from a science fiction book I'm writing."

> Dragon's ear and druid's spear
> Protects you while the *Dworns are here
> The winds of wrath chill cold the cloth
> That drapes her shape from the fangs of fear.
> I love you my love
> Please taketh this heart which I bear
> O heal my sorrow
> Weareth my arms like a charm
> Through the dales of your doom
> Our lives are merely trees of possibilities.
> DRAGON'S EAR by Marc Bolan

Marc's footnote:
Dworn: Machinery of war; a bronze frame with wheels of white ivory and the horns of a gazelle for steering, so sayeth Agadinmar.

Marc Bolan, 1972:
Everything I do is poetry to music.

> . . . Tree wizard Puretongue
> The digger of holes
> The swan king
> The Elf lord
> The eater of souls
> Lithon the black
> The rider of stars
> Tyrannosaurus Rex
> The eater of cars.
>
> From SUNEYE by Marc Bolan

June Bolan:
Tyrannosaurus Rex. It came about because, in fact, it's a very easy name; it's phonetic if you think about it.

> . . . A big cat like a t — tyrannosaurus going to Lilliput
> The ensemble make a tiny rumble, the celloist solos
> From STRANGE ORCHESTRAS
> by Marc Bolan

June Bolan:
But it's a word that people in England cannot look at and pronounce. Ask Annie Nightingale; you ask her to say it. She can't even say it now, not to this day. It just became too heavy to handle. Radio, the Press — it became all sorts of odd combinations. Marc was all ideas; he just needed people to implement them for him. So we called T. Rex.

Tony Visconti:
From GET IT ON onwards Marc realised that I knew — that

I understood the T. Rex sound. I had a lot of say about what was to go on top of the track, but, of course, I'll go down on record as saying that I never had much say about the actual content of the music.

Steve Currie:
Bass player with T. Rex
There never was a group, never from the start. What we used to do was, Marc would give me a call and say: "I've written some songs. Can you come round?"
I'd go round to his flat and he'd play an acoustic lead while I'd work out the bass lines. Then we'd take them into the studios; it was just a case of rehearsing then in his flat before doing them in the studios. We used to work out the bass lines between us; very simple ideas if you listen to it. His best stuff was very simple. Every note was worked out and calculated. And that's the way we worked. But the whole thing was Marc Bolan. It was never T. Rex. He was T. Rex.

Tony Visconti:
I was very taken in by T. Rex. I dedicated my life to T. Rex, for about the first five years.

Simone French, *Evening News*, June 23rd 1970:
How T. Rex got it right at 4 a.m. . . .
By twenty to four in the morning you're getting pretty nervous for them. They are over-run on studio time; a jumpy, half-calm is squeezing us all; and it's just not sounding right. There are faint jokes: "Just one note I didn't like", more cigarettes, only the lighter won't work properly, and there's nothing to quench the stale taste in our mouths except the last, slag inch of cold coffee.
They do one more take. The ninth. At ten minutes to four we suddenly know that that's it. It's funky. It's the T. Rex sound.
Marc Bolan says: "You can keep that one." His voice is hoarse.
Whatever you might think, we haven't over-dramatised the scene. These are the sort of sweaty hang-ups a group goes through, putting an LP together.
"You must do it, and do it again. Until it's right," said Tony Visconti, T. Rex's producer. "Nine out of ten records are made that way."

Tony Visconti:
We were extremely compatible in a professional sense. We grew together. We were both penniless at the same time; we were both unknown at the same time; and we both got famous at the same time.

Simone French, *Evening News:*
The pressures aren't only for musical perfection. It costs £25 an hour during the day, £30 at night, to hire a recording studio.
You can reckon on eight sessions of eight hours at least, to record an LP. Plus two sessions to reduce the length of it, and another four to get the sound balance correct.

That's £2,000 before you pay for the tapes or anything else.

Tony Visconti:
When RIDE A WHITE SWAN became hit number two, which was the highest it ever got, we were in the studio making T. Rex; it was the first album called T. Rex and Marc and I had about five pounds between us in our pockets. We still hadn't received any royalties from RIDE A WHITE SWAN. It was just happening, and here we were, the same two geezers who'd started out a few years earlier with this Tyrannosaurus Rex thing in our minds, and we struck gold, you know. That was a fantastic feeling. We were walking about a foot off the ground the whole day; it almost halted our recording session completely.

Mick O'Halloran:
They were memorable says.

Mickey Finn:
Mick, me and Marc were very close.

Simone French, *Evening News:*
. . . there are only five top-class recording studios in London and ten which range from good to mediocre. With so many groups turning out records, you're lucky to get recording time at all.

Tony Visconti:
We used to go down from Trident Studios, where we recorded mostly. We used to walk down to Cranks, the vegetarian restaurant, just a short walk from Trident.

Mick O'Halloran:
At that time he was a very strong vegetarian. He never ate meat; couldn't stand the smell of it. He wouldn't even eat eggs at that time.

Tony Visconti:
We could only afford a hot pot, you know, a hot roll and a cup of jasmine tea.

Simone French, *Evening News:*
"Take two," says the dispassionate voice in the control room. Below, in the dimly lit studio, seen through a double glass window, T. Rex are two lonely intent people.
It'll mean nine takes to get it right, each one listened to again with a sort of religious rapture by Marc and Mickey.

Tony Visconti:
There was absolutely no presence of drugs in those days.

June Bolan:
He never took acid in his life.

Tony Visconti:
We were very pure and poor.

Eric Hall:
The drugs side, I've got to be totally honest about. I heard, and I hear from people that he took drugs very heavily, and I assume, knowing Marc as well as I did, he did take drugs. But I never saw him. I was never a witness.

June Bolan:
He never smoked dope because people in England always rolled grass or hash into tobacco and because it was thought to be anti-social not to smoke — I mean, if one went to a house, everybody smoked, everybody took acid in sixty-eight. It was the peace-love-hippy-trippy days. Nobody said no. It just wasn't done.

Tony Visconti:
In those days you'd walk into anybody's recording session and there'd be loads of cocaine about. That was the drug for those days and we all had a little go, a little flirtation with it. But I was one of the closest people to Marc, and I can honestly say he really shied away from drugs. He never smoked marijuana.

June Bolan:
So what he used to do, he just used to hold his breath. He literally didn't know how to smoke; he didn't know how to get it into his body, so he just used to hold it for about three minutes and then pass it on so as not to lose face.

Tony Visconti:
But he was very partial to champagne and brandy. Someone did spike him once at a party. They put some acid in a drink of his and he had an involuntary LSD trip which apparently was horrible; a pretty nasty thing to do to anybody.

> ...And me, I fought a great worm
> Sent to taste my jaguar feet
> And used his skin to make my wings begin
> I sussed and stole a scene from Icarus
> And flew us above some uncooked meat
> A plastic hook pierced through my instep
> I flew too near his Brutus heart.
> From THE SCENESCOF DYNASTY
> by Marc Bolan

June Bolan, as told to Danae Brook, *Evening News*:
Marc was one-directional. He wanted to be famous so he made it happen. Like a blinkered horse he knew exactly where he was going, and how to find the people who would help him get there.

Eric Hall:
He knew the right person. Shrewd.

... He used to say in interviews: "I'm just a punk. An East End punk."

Tony Visconti:
He had some funny ideas. He had this sort of philosophy that if he went out as Marc Bolan he wouldn't get as much work as if he went out as T. Rex, you know? It was silly. He couldn't see the wood for the trees. Everyone knew it was Marc Bolan and his band and he called his band T. Rex.

June Bolan:
He was destined and fated to do what he did.

Danae Brook, *Evening News*:
It was Marc's most successful and creative period. He was utilising all his talents — and, as they both had always known would happen, he was suddenly on the crest of the wave of teenage adulation which thrust T. Rex into the fore-front of the music scene in the early Seventies.

Tony Visconti:
There was vicious competition in the early days when Bolan was happening and Bowie had his big hit before Bolan: SPACE ODDITY. I remember they were always in this bitter competition. I was producing them both at that time and I got Marc to play on one of David's records. He did a lovely guitar solo.... That was the only time they ever got to any kind of harmony, apart from the last TV show that Marc did with David Bowie. But they were never really friendly. I mean David's very open. David would love to have been friends with Marc.

June Bolan:
Marc was a total Libran; a creator. That was his life.... He'd sit in the sitting room, reading; just music papers or something. Then suddenly, he'd get up and run into the music room and grab a pen and a piece of paper and just scribble away in that manic writing of his. He'd never say a word. I'd hear the chords trying to fit the words, and then I'd hear the tape go, then the door slam and I knew he was really getting down to what he was doing. And maybe half an hour later I'd hear: "Come and listen to it. What d'you think?" I'd listen and if I didn't like it I'd say so. And he'd just shriek and say: "Well, you don't have to say things like

that!" And I'd say: "Well, if you don't want to know, don't ask me." Then he'd slam the door. A little while later, he'd come back in and he would have changed it to the sort of thing one had suggested. But you could never say that. You'd say: "Oh, that's wonderful. That's really good." And he'd say: "Yes. It needed something like that." But he was always a very quick worker. He was never one of those people who'd sit for days and days, working out lines and words. It just happened, like a force flowing out of him.

Steve Turner, *Beat Instrumental*, Nov. 1971:

In his new Maida Vale home Marc has a music room where he puts down ideas on tape. The room itself has posters of Jimi Hendrix hanging on the walls while guitars lay around on the floor. A Brennel tape recorder and an organ of an unknown make are the only other pieces of equipment in the room. Describing how he works Marc said: "I play about for a couple of hours before I move into new dimensions where I'm being very creative. I record everything then."

Steve Currie:

He knew where he was going. He was different in those days. He had the drive; it was before he got into alcohol and other things. It's very difficult to put into words, but to meet somebody who knows exactly where they're going...! He sat there in November 1970 endlessly writing in Ladbroke Grove, and he knew exactly what he was going to do and there was nothing that was going to stop him. It was sheer energy and that's why I had so much respect for him. And he died in the midst of a silly argument we had. Well ...

And I'll skip with you
in the midnight blue
and carve fluting pipes
for you to play on.
                    From THE FRIENDS by Marc Bolan

He wouldn't listen, that was his problem. He had the ability; you could have bunged him into the finest guitarist in the world and say teach him for a week. And Marc would have been a two hundred per cent better guitarist, but unfortunately Marc never listened. . . . But that was the thing that made him successful in the first place.

Tony Visconti:

He was very reluctant to take any musical advice. He would sit with me after I had written the arrangements, and I had to play all the parts to him. When we played the backing track, he had to listen and we would only proceed when he was sure it would work. He would ask me to change a few notes, or take a few out, which was good discipline for me; being classically trained, I tend to go over the top like any other arranger or composer. But when we did GET IT ON Marc couldn't see strings on it at all. We had string players down there for two other songs, and I just sketched this very little string part, just putting a high, very sustained note over the whole song, here and there, just a moving high part. We had half an hour left and I said: "Come on, Marc. Let's try this out." It was the first time we didn't sit down and talk about an arrangement. I went over his head and just did it. He said: "It doesn't need strings." I said: "Come on, Marc. Look. I've written it, I've copied it all out. Let's do it." Finally he agreed and we did it. And he said: "Hey! It works! It works! Great." And that was it. GET IT ON had strings on it and virtually very single afterwards had strings on it too.

John Peel:

His fans found his move to the 'electric sound' a bit difficult, because it was obviously a step in the jump towards *Top of the Pops*, which is a unique process.

B. P. Fallon:

He managed to alienate a limited amount of people by doing that, and that saddened him I think.

Marc Bolan, 1972:

I've always been a better electric guitarist than an acoustic guitarist anyway. I just wanted people to know that.

John Peel:

I didn't enjoy it a great deal myself.

B. P. Fallon:

But then a whole new bunch of folk appeared and merged in with the large majority of people who had been there before, so, in fact, people weren't lost.

Steve Turner, *Beat Instrumental*, Nov. 1971:

Marc has a total of nine guitars laying around his room of music. He has two Fender Stratocasters, one Fender Telecaster with a Gibson pick-up, one 1952 Les Paul, one SG special (Les Paul), one Gibson Flying Arrow, one Gibson acoustic and one Epiphone acoustic.

Marc Bolan, 1972:

When we started in '67 everyone was doing Cream, Hendrix, and it was very much hard Rock. The only way I could break through was to be something completely opposite. By the time it got to be 1970 everyone was playing acoustic. Had I not done what I'm doing now, I would have ended up like Cat Stevens which is not what I want to be. I'd much rather be a cock Rock star, 'cause I can do whatever I want to do.

Tony Visconti:

Whenever I did tell Marc, whenever I echoed the criticism that was being thrown at him, which was that his records were beginning to sound alike, Marc would say that I was sounding like a Press man and say: "Nonsense! I am always progressing. You heard my guitar playing on the last record." I'd say: "Yes. But it's not only the guitar. The guitar playing is fine. You must take some time off and learn some new chords." I mean, I used to tune his guitar for him quite often and I'd show him a new chord in a song, an obvious chord, like to go from A major to D major you would need an A7th. His idea of an A7th was just lifting a finger off a string so that it was just an A major with a foreign note in it, which was charming. It worked several times.

John Peel:
The reason I hadn't seen Marc for five or six years was simply because, when he released GET IT ON, he brought the record along to John Walters (who produces my BBC programme) so that we could play it on the radio, as we had done with all his previous ones. We listened to it and thought, well frankly, if this was Marc we wouldn't play it because we wanted to remain honest to our listeners and to myself.
Marc saw this as a betrayal and from that day I have only met him once.

Marc Bolan, 1972:
I'm not limited. I don't like people that put me in a corner. I really resented that.

Keith Altham, *Look Now*, 1970:
It seems you either have to love him or hate him but I like him, which must make some sort of sense. . . .

June Bolan, as told to Danae Brook, *Evening News*:
He had that indefinable something which makes your spine tingle and the hairs on the back of your neck stand up.

Keith Altham, *Look Now*:
. . . maybe it is that the truth often exists between two extremes and that at least would appear to be the case for the defence of Marc Bolan.

B. P. Fallon:
He was no saint; not a grievous sinner either.

Tony Visconti:
When that record, RIDE A WHITE SWAN, made number two, we nearly passed out. I mean, that was one moment that Marc couldn't cope with success. He lost his equilibrium for a little while there. Then all of a sudden, about two weeks later, he realised he was a star at last.

Marc Bolan, Nov. 1972:
I have no choice but to see myself as a teenage idol. I like living. It's a part of my life and I have to go through it and enjoy it sometimes. I don't like the fact that I can't walk down the street anymore or really go out. But that's part of what you have to pay. I like the freedom that it's given me artistically; to do whatever I want. The money, of course, helps.

Tony Visconti:
He became a real recluse in actual fact. He rarely stepped out of his flat, once he got successful; he rarely walked anywhere; he was always in limousines. He never related to street people, or the use of hard drugs, or poverty, or anything like that.
He lived and created his own environment and had everyone around him add to it. You had to nurture his fantasies and help them along. You could never burst his bubble; Marc would never want his bubble to be burst.

June Bolan:
Without a doubt he loved himself. I mean totally. But then we both believed that we were very special. I still do.

B. P. Fallon:
He was extraordinarily pretty.

Tony Visconti:
He lived in his own world, definitely. The only walk I ever took with him was once from my flat to the off-licence, and I had to go with one of his bodyguards. He thought it was really great. It was about the first time he had walked three blocks. We bought three bottles of wine. He was recognised by the cashier. Big deal! Well, the bodyguard was unnecessary, but it was the longest walk I had ever taken with him, besides the earlier days when we used to record at Trident Studios.

Keith Altham, *Look Now*:
There are those who point with derision to his employment of make-up or eye-glitter and they are usually the same pack who can be found applauding the outrageous Alice or the camping Bowie.

Marc Bolan, as told to David Neill, *Record Weekly*:
I wear what I like, what I'm comfortable in; it helps me to relax. Those guys wore dark suits because they thought it made them invisible. I don't say what they should wear; clothes are not that important.

Keith Altham, *Look Now*:
Bolan is pop. Sometimes fun — seldom heavy and more often playful. What began as a series of grunts back in the days of Presley, Richard, Lee Lewis and Eddie Cochran, is being transformed today into a new poetry of laughter and fantasy by the 'Little bopper'.

Marc Bolan, as told to David Neill, *Record Weekly*:
I wear women's shoes because I like them and they are cheap. People can wear what they want. I wear what helps me to function in a hard society.

Tony Visconti:
I'm sure he was bisexual, but, you know, I never caught him in the act.

Trucking down by the roadside
Met a man with starhide
He said: "Boy, wouldn't you like to look?"
But could it give me love
Gimme little love
Gimme little love from God's heart
And then we'll walk.
From BELTANE WALK by Marc Bolan

June Bolan:
Just say he was ambitious.

Bopping down by the whirlpool
I met a girl she was God's tool
I said: "Girl, wouldn't you like to Rock?"
But could it give me love
Gimme little love
Gimme little love from God's heart
And then we'll walk.
From BELTANE WALK by Marc Bolan

Tony Visconti:
I'm sure Marc was bisexual but Bowie beat him to it by announcing in the Press officially that he was bisexual. And I think Marc was a bit bitter about that.

June Bolan:
All this thing about him being gay in the papers came up later, because it was fashionable to say you were. But he actually loathed making love to men.

Marc Bolan, as told to Jan Iles, *Record Mirror*, Feb. 1st 1975:
I'm bisexual but I believe I'm heterosexual, 'cos I definitely like boobs. I always wish I were a hundred per cent gay; it's much easier, but not much fun. You have the best of both worlds. But I think if you're gay or whatever, you have just as much fun. Anyway I checked it out and I prefer chicks.

Walking down by the West wind
I met a boy he was my friend
I said: "Boy, we could sing it too."
And we do give us love
Give us little love
Give us little love from your hearts
Give us love
Give us little love from your hearts
And then we'll walk.
From BELTANE WALK by Marc Bolan

Tony Visconti:
I'm sure he had one or two affairs with men, but he saw it also as a terrible loss of face, in the fact that Bowie beat him to it publicly.

Steve Currie:
I think his make-up was AC/DC; I mean, sexually he liked

women but there was still the other side where he preferred the company of men.

Met a man, he was nice
Said his name was Paradise
Didn't realise at the time
That his face and mind were mine
Hippy Gumbo, he's no good
Chop him up for firewood.

It seemed good and it seemed right
That I should dig him all the night
But in the morning with the sun
He pulled an automatic gun
He blew my soul, he blew my brain
He split, I could not do the same.

Hippy Gumbo, he's no good
Chop him up for firewood
Hippy Gumbo, he's no good
Chop him up and burn the wood.
HIPPY GUMBO by Marc Bolan

June Bolan:
You probably wouldn't understand the words to the song, but I know exactly what they mean. It was about a man he was in love with when he was fifteen years old; whom he lived with for six months.

Steve Harley, Leader of *Cockney Rebel*:
The ones who really know the truth might be the only ones who got that involved — involved that closely with him.

Gloria Jones:
Singer, Record Producer and mother of Marc Bolan's son, Rolan.
No one really knows him; he was an individual.

June Bolan:
We lived together, virtually for twenty-four hours a day, for three and a half years. We had the cold-water flat and the one below that we had expanded. We had two floors of the same house and it was £11 a week. We had knocked a hole in the wall, so there was a huge room; there was the upstairs room, the little music room that we had sound-proofed with egg boxes and things, and the kitchen, cold water, still no hot water. One morning we woke and he said: "Fancy getting married?"

You're so sweet
You're so fine
I want you all and everything
Just to be mine

Cos you're my baby
Cos you're my love
Girl I'm just a jeepster
For your love

You slide so good
With bones so fair
You've got the universe
Reclining in your hair

Just like a car
You're pleasing to behold
I'll call you Jaguar
If I may be so bold

The wild winds blow
Upon your frozen cheeks
The way you flip your hip
It always makes me weak

Your motivation
Is so sweet
Your vibrations
Are burning up my feet

Girl I'm just a jeepster
For your love
Girl I'm just a vampire
For your love

I'm gonna suck you.

JEEPSTER by Marc Bolan

I was twenty-seven and I thought, well, why not? I haven't done it before and we'd been living together for three and a half years and it really made absolutely no difference to our lives. So we went to the Kensington Register Office and said: "How do you do it? What do you do?" They told us that you pay so much deposit and get this special licence, or you wait three weeks and pay half the price, and we said No. He had a bit of money left; he was getting Performing Right Society cheques and things like that, so we had some money. We still had the van — we went to the wedding in the van — so he said we would get a special licence. And three days later we were married.

Mickey Finn:
I went to the wedding.

Steve Currie:
I never had much to do with June.

B. P. Fallon:
I think she's fantastic.

Gloria Jones:
I don't really know June. I only knew Marc.

Steve Currie:
She was just Marc's old lady.

B. P. Fallon:
I think she was incredibly important to both Marc's career

and to Marc as a person; she knows him very well.

Steve Currie:
She used to come on the road.

Mickey Finn:
June did all the accounts. She used to drive us around to all the gigs — and fix all the punctures!

June Bolan:
I wouldn't let anyone else drive him to gigs. I went to every single gig that he went to.

B. P. Fallon:
She's a very good hustler.

Steve Currie:
She never really did anything to me; never shot me down.

B. P. Fallon:
She can come over as being very hard sometimes, but inside she's as soft as a fruitcake.

Steve Currie:
She always had towels ready when we came off stage; she was always looking after the welfare of the band; she made sure the dressing room was cool. She was very good to the band.

B. P. Fallon:
I think she was a very, very important balance for Marc. She taught him a fair bit about logic. I mean, at one point, he didn't have much logic in him, in terms of so-called practical things.

Danae Brook, *Evening News*:
When I met them at this time, about 1971, they looked almost identical. Like astral twins. Each wraith-thin, large-eyed, with dark curly hair that did not so much cascade as fly out from the pale pre-Raphaelite faces like the wings of a bird.

Steve Currie:
I first met Marc through the good old *Melody Maker*.

Mick O'Halloran:
Marc decided he wanted a proper band, so they advertised for a bass player.

Steve Currie:
There was this little ad in the *Melody Maker* saying: Bass

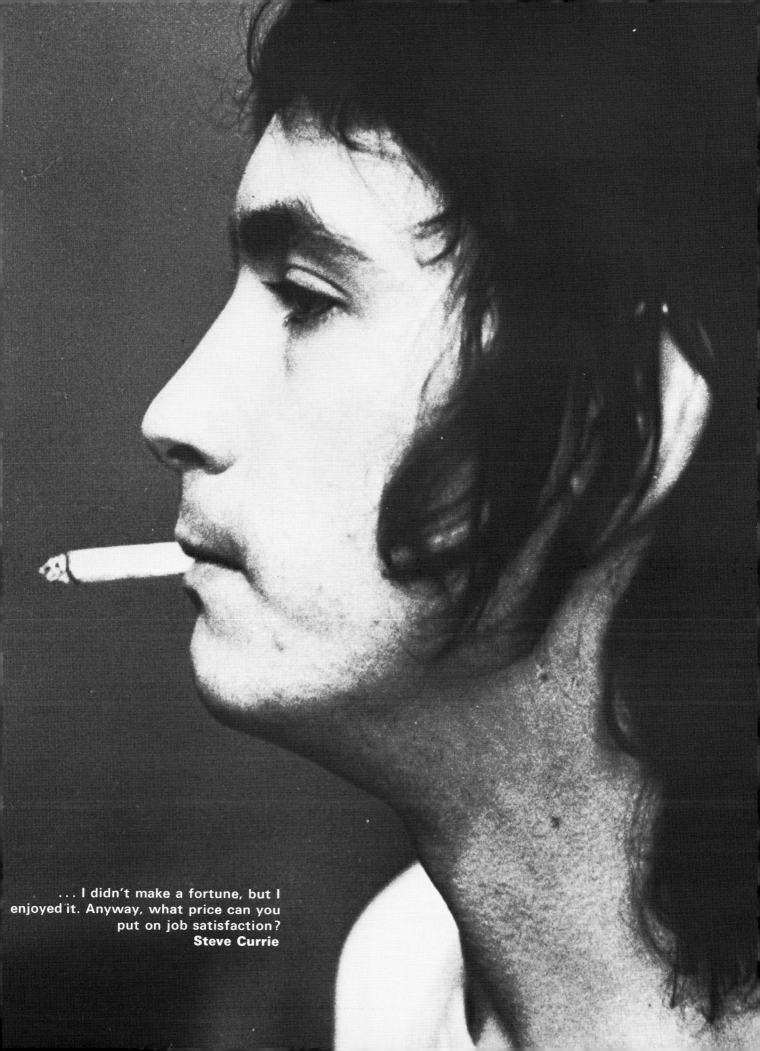

... I didn't make a fortune, but I enjoyed it. Anyway, what price can you put on job satisfaction?
Steve Currie

Tokio station 1973. L to R Jack Green, Tony Howard, Mickey Finn, Alphi O'Leary, Marc, Bill Legend.

player wanted to augment guitarist and percussionist. Not even a box. It just said: Apply at so-and-so address.

Mick O'Halloran:
We auditioned some bass players, all sorts of people, at a little place near the Elephant; a school hall. And we had Steve Currie come along; he came along with his wife.

Steve Currie:
So I went along to this rehearsal room and we really got on, you know. We played for about twenty minutes and he said: "Well, we'll give you a call." And that was it.

Mick O'Halloran:
That was the chap that Marc and June chose, because they said that he had a lot of balls coming along there to audition with his wife, you know; like he didn't really care whether he got the job or not. He said he'd done it for his own thing.

Steve Currie:
It was a very strange meeting because I'd always been a rocker; I'd come from an eleven-piece jazz-Rock band so I thought, Jesus Christ, jingle-jangle type! But that was the point where he decided to change his career from being a mediocre star who loved flowers, to carving out a Rock 'n' Roll career for himself.

Mick O'Halloran:
He was a very good bass player, for that period of time. So Steve got the job.

Steve Currie:
It was easy work then; we used to do two sides, a forty-five-minute set. I wasn't a Tyrannosaurus Rex fan. It just wasn't my cup of tea. But when Marc explained the direction he wanted to go, and I went round to his flat — he was living in Ladbroke Grove at that time — he played me some tapes that gave a general idea of what he was going to do,

knock that hippy thing on the head, I said: "Great. Sign me up." The first single I did was HOT LOVE of course.

Tony Visconti:
Around the HOT LOVE and GET IT ON period, when the money was there — of course it was there — we were spending a longer time in the studio and it was noticeable that we were getting better sounds and we were innovating things.

Steve Currie:
I mean, he was an amazing rhythm guitarist. If you listen to HOT LOVE and GET IT ON, they're classics of really four to the bar, straight foot-tappers.

Tony Visconti:
It was just an unbelievable period of my life. And, of course, Marc's. It was just unbelievable that feeling of growing more and more successful. I don't know at what age Marc began, but I did my first professional gig when I was twelve. When you finally strike gold it's amazing, you know. And when it's something you believe in, that's even more amazing.

Peter Cole, *Evening Times*, Jan. 28th 1972:
During the week they are at school. But on Saturdays and Sundays they gather together at the altar, a band of about 200 teenage and sub-teenage girls paying homage to the diminutive god figure who may or may not be upstairs behind that window.
Marc Bolan, pop super-star, never appears. He hears the girls chanting: "Come on, Marc! We know you're up there!" He smiles and waits for them to go away.

Tony Visconti:
There was a point when he actually was selling, with HOT LOVE, twenty-eight thousand a day. That was a number one record for seven weeks.

B. P. Fallon:
On stage, then it was good. It was never bettered by anybody.

Peter Cole, *Evening Times*:
After the shows are over they queue up outside Marc's door, longing for a glimpse of their hero. Sometimes he invites them into his dressing room, two at a time. He presents them with a signed photograph, gives them the obligatory peck, and out they go, happy for weeks and months to come.

B. P. Fallon:
When all the riots started and the kids went crazy, he had fantastic control of that. I remember one gig; the whole place was shaking and the manager came out and said:

"Unless everyone sits down, the show's cancelled. People are going to get hurt." And from his point of view, the theatre manager was talking logic. So Marc took the mike and said: "No one's going to get hurt, are they?" And everyone shouted back: "No!" And nobody did, which was extraordinary, really, because it was pandemonium. He could quieten an audience down, and he could raise it up again.

June Bolan:
He didn't stop planning what he was going to do next. And that's how it went on, always.

Tony Visconti:
We enjoyed about two years of creative success.

B. P. Fallon:
When you think of his influence, I mean, he made people like the Stones get off their arses and worry about their position. And the reason he did that was because he was getting so incredibly strong.

June Bolan:
He worked the whole time.

Steve Currie:
Marc was a city boy; he loved the glamour, the glitter, the limousines.

B. P. Fallon
You can tell how strong a Rock 'n' Roll band is sometimes, by when you look into the audience and all the people look like the star. And that happened. It was incredible.

June Bolan:
We hadn't had a holiday for years.

Tony Visconti:
In those days I existed solely for Marc Bolan. I was doing the Strawbs, I was doing Ralph McTell, but I knew my interests were in Marc.

June Bolan:
Our first holiday was magnificent. We went to the West Indies, Barbados, just the two of us; no roadies, no personal assistants. Can you imagine? From the Portobello Road to the West Indies, just the two of us, holding hands!
When we got there, I rented a car and the hotel was just wonderful. As a matter of fact, it turned out to be the hotel that Elton's mother had stayed at two weeks previously, so they knew all about us and treated us really nicely. We stayed two weeks; really healthy little things, brown as berries. Marc wanted me to go water-skiing, but I didn't

Someone said to me "So you've lost a friend." Nah, no way. Bole's still about, he always will be. He's looking over your shoulder now reading this, betcha. Grinning away, y'know?
We're still in touch. It's simply a matter of realigning your communication area.
I'll tell you — Bole's rocking, rocking more than ever.
Bless you, Marc, you ol' tart ... and thank you, too.
And don't forget to reserve me a good seat ...
B. P. Fallon

swim in those days. Neither did Marc, only I didn't know that, and although he hated sport of any description, I believed him when he said he could. So I said I'd go water-skiing if he went as well, and very bravely, he said okay. So this beautiful six foot five 'spade' — wonderful man, one of the Olympic team — he has a go at teaching Marc. Next thing he knows, Marc is up to his neck in water with the skis up in the air. He tried and he tried but after about half an hour of having his arms pulled out of their sockets and just getting his bottom wet, he gave up. He tried, his hands all aching, but do you think he could stand up on those skis? No way. But he was so humiliated; I mean, he always had to succeed and to be beaten by two lumps of wood and a speedboat was more than he could take. He stormed out of the water and said: "You go and bloody do it. It's a stupid sport. Who wants to stand on two planks of wood? I hope you realise I'll probably never be able to play the guitar again. Look at my hands. Ruined!" In actual fact, there wasn't a mark on them. But all afternoon he sat on the beach holding his hands up at the sun in the hope they would heal. But to make matters worse, I was able to water-ski straight off. I've never done it before. Must have good balance.... They were a wonderful two weeks.

I'm gonna dance with my princess
By the light of a magical moon
As I go along my way
I say hey hey
I'm gonna talk with the elders
And tell all of our hearts
That is good
I'll barefoot dance with my baby
By the light of a magical moon.
When I slay the darkest day
Then we can play
Till that deep and joyous day
We'll dance and pray.
BY THE LIGHT OF A MAGICAL MOON
by Marc Bolan

Marc and I came back from Barbados on the Monday, and on the Wednesday we were going back with Ringo. Just the three of us. Ringo was very close to Marc then; I mean, he was like a father to us; he taught us loads of things; a wonderful person. Maureen (Ringo's wife) didn't want to go with us because she hated the sun and Ringo had never had a holiday without her. (They were still married at this time.)
So there we were, the three of us in the first-class compartment on the plane. There were eight people altogether and they showed a funny Woody Allen film. The three of us were soon pretty drunk, because this was in the days before the Jumbo jet and it was a fourteen-hour flight, with only one stop in Antigua. We were legless, absolutely pie-eyed, because they bring you free drinks, brandy and champagne. We were watching this film with headsets; the others in the compartment were really grumpy bats out of hell and didn't want to watch the film; they wanted to read. But we were making so much noise that this old chap came over and rapped us on the head with his book, took our headsets off and told us to shut up and behave ourselves. Marc just blew a raspberry or something. We

were really stoned. This man went and told the captain, pilot or whatever — I used to call him the driver — so the driver comes back ready to reprimand us. I mean, we had these headsets on and you can't hear yourself, you see. We were shrieking at each other and at the film, and must have sounded like a load of banshees to everyone else. The driver came back and said he had a complaint about the noise, and while he was saying this, he was looking up at the screen and he started to laugh. Ringo stood up and the captain came and sat next to Marc. The four of us were hysterical and the man who had complained to the captain in the first place, was laughing himself into a stupor with the rest of us. It was absolutely hysterical all the way to Barbados. We spent another two weeks there with Ringo, Marc and me. But Ringo had this strange skin complaint; he used to have to wear those funny little cardboard noses and a hat and dark glasses and a tee shirt that he used to roll up to his elbows. Marc and I have skins that just go absolutely black in the sun, but poor Ringo would sit there with his socks on because he used to get burnt ankles. We spent our time eating, drinking and going to clubs. It was wonderful for Ringo because he'd never really had a holiday privately because of his involvement with the Beatle thing. That was our first posh holiday; to go twice in a month ...! It wasn't that I ever thought: "Gosh, I'm so proud of you for having done so well." It was just that I always knew that's what he'd do. It sounds an odd thing to say. But true.

David Neill, *Record Weekly*:
"Success can happen overnight," he says, "but when you've made it, you've still got to cope with it."

Mickey Finn:
The success was like a wedge; it drove us apart.

June Bolan:
We would have champagne. I mean, at first it was wonderful to be famous and have girls coming up in the street and grabbing hair and things like that and then it turned out to be an absolute drag. We moved house to Clarendon Gardens and we spent one whole summer on our hands and knees, because it had huge French windows, this house; it was either that or have the curtains closed throughout the whole summer, because the house was inundated with girls the whole time.

Steve Currie:
If you can understand, he had too many fans. Fans liking you was the last of your worries. It was survival, rather than half a dozen tasty little things coming up to you. It was just a blanket thing.

David Neill, *Record Weekly*:
Once when they booked a hotel too near the theatre it was besieged for hours by hundreds of fans.
It is some time now since any group got the sort of audience reaction stirred up by the insistent rhythms of T. Rex. One theatre manager threatened to stop the show

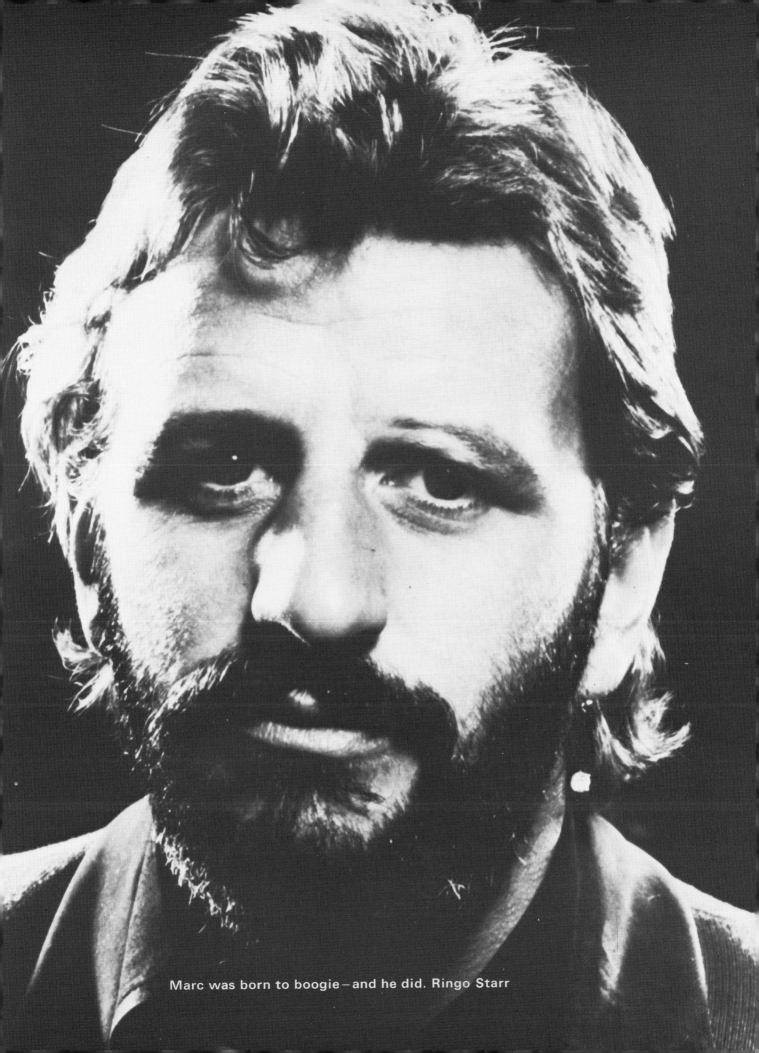

Marc was born to boogie—and he did. Ringo Starr

because someone might get hurt. After Marc had made sure that no one would be hurt, and had offered to pay for any damage, the show went on.

June Bolan:
We lived very close to Regent's Park Zoo. We had a thing about Guy the Gorilla; he was a real friend of ours. I've got huge posters and if I go to see Guy, he goes ridiculous if he sees me. That's through years of knowing him. Marc and I used to go once or twice a week, regular as clockwork; take cauliflower and things like that. We were just two people who lived in Maida Vale visiting the Zoo, as far as we were concerned. But one day, we saw all these coaches outside; it must have been a school outing or something. Anyway, we were just standing there looking at Guy, when suddenly we heard this voice cry out: "Look! it's Marc! Marc Bolan!" I turned round and there was this whole coach load of pubescent girls running at us. Marc just looked at me, grabbed my hand and we fled. We never went back to the Zoo again.

Mick O'Halloran:
We arrived at Exeter University; it was sort of — you know, one of these Grand Ball type of things. When Marc did his spot, the audience just rose out from the floor (because they used to sit on the floor) and cheered, and clapped, and demanded more. I'd never experienced anything like it. Then he did another number which just left everybody, like — in amazement! Unbelievable show!

Marc Bolan, as told to Peter Cole, *Evening Times*:
It's not really me wielding power. It's the audience wanting to have it done to them.

Adrian:
A devoted fan of Marc Bolan
The moment he walked on stage I just stared at him the whole time. You had to look at him.

Mick O'Halloran:
Everywhere that we seemed to be going all these — what we called at the time — freaks followed him. I mean, they weren't obvious freaks; they were human beings. But it was like a cult. Unbelievable. Everywhere we went, sold out!

Tony Visconti:
When I used to travel with the group, there was a period when I really had to virtually follow them from country to country to record them; they were so hot. One of the albums, I think it was ELECTRIC WARRIOR, we made in four different countries. Some tracks were recorded in Denmark, some were recorded in France and some were recorded in Los Angeles. JEEPSTER was recorded in New York. Two different cities. I was following the group around.

Catch a bright star and place it on your forehead,
Say a few spells and there you go....
From RIDE A WHITE SWAN by Marc Bolan

Danae Brook, *Evening News*:
They were living through a dynamic and formative time in social history. The spirit of adventure and cultural change which prevailed then enabled imaginative ideas to fall on fertile ground. Marc Bolan was full of ideas and it was his time.

Tony Visconti:
I always had a feeling that if Marc would have learned something about technique, which he never had much of ... he had the charisma, he had the guts, he had the leadership, he had almost everything except technique and actual academic background for some of the things he wanted to do. Like his film he made with Ringo; it had its moments. You could see the man had imagination but, you know, you should go and study something about cinematography; you should take a course in it or read some books on it.

Marc Bolan as told to Steve Turner, *Beat Instrumental*, Oct. 1972:
The reason for this film (*Born to Boogie*) being so important is because it is a real film. Basically the film is about the best bits of the concerts, with bits and pieces in general. There is a lot that's funny in it too. I mean, it's really very funny. There's really no theme; it's audio-visual space age Rock 'n' Roll. It's about nothing. There's no story. It's centred around me and the group.

Steve Currie:
The film *Born to Boogie* was really a total ego trip. I just played the Wembley concert and wouldn't have anything to do with the film. There was Marc and Ringo, clashing their egos, trying to impress each other.

Left. Marc speaking to DJ Jeff Dexter; this photograph was taken by Adrian a few days before the fatal accident. It was the last time Adrian saw him.

*The late Guy of London Zoo; he died of a heart attack,
aged thirty-two, on June 8th 1978.*

*Ringo Starr, B. P. Fallon and Marc on the film set of
"Born to Boogie".*

Ringo Starr, Director of *Born to Boogie*, as told to Tony Norman, *New Musical Express*:

I phoned him up one day and said, "Come and see me. I've got this idea. See what you think, yes or no." But through that meeting we got friendly. Then I heard he was going to be filmed at his Wembley concert. Well, Apple has a film company so I said: "Why don't you let me do it? I'm yer pal." he said: "Okay, we'll do it together."

Marc Bolan, as told to Steve Turner:

What it is though, is the best of the concerts and a lot of me and Ringo goofing around and a couple of studio things, bits and pieces stuck together in a way that's stimulating to the body and the soul. I hope. I mean, I get off on it.

Steve Currie:

The only thing I had to do, which was the biggest laugh, was to re-do a bass line at Apple Studios. There was this big stand-up row between Marc and Tony (Visconti) because Marc was out of tune at the Wembley concert, and he refused to believe it.

Tony Visconti:

I found the best way to confront him would be in private. If there was a studio full of people, it would be war. He only really knew about six or seven chords. If I pointed out he was playing the wrong chords in front of other musicians, it would be hell. In the early days I just let him do what he wanted; he was so avant-garde; he was just busting his guitar to pieces on the T. Rex sessions. But when he was doing straight Rock 'n' Roll, like GET IT ON and all that, I had to definitely point him in a few directions there. He really didn't know how certain things were done. There was a period where he did go to Eric Clapton's house a few times and watch the master at work. He picked up a little bit from him, but he wouldn't admit it.

Marc Bolan, as told to Anne Nightingale in *Petticoat*:

Financially, *Born to Boogie* was a gamble, because we put our own money into it and, had it flopped, it would have made a serious dent! The other risks involved were that of critical acclaim. In fact the film didn't get good reviews. It was slated by everyone. But they all put it down for the wrong reasons, which is why it didn't bother me. The critics put it down for not being a masterpiece as a film. But it was made for T. Rex fans, for no one else. That's what upset the critics.

Tony Visconti:

He told me once that critics only heard him one time; that was the first time he was slagged and he quickly built up a defence against being slagged. First bad review he read, he wept. He was depressed for days. Then, as soon

A still from "Born to Boogie"; Ringo Starr is in the bearskin.

as he pulled out of it, he never got depressed again. He just said: "Oh, critics are a load of shit. They don't make records. I'm the man in the studio. I'm the one who's making.' ... I happen to share his opinion, you know.

Steve Harley:
They never understood him; the Press just couldn't. If you think of the music press, the writers, the reporters in England, he was beyond them; he was above them all in that his mind was so close to madness, they would have had to have been imaginative people to have understood him, literally to have understood; not just to have understood his meaning, but to have understood the person and sympathised with him. But they don't have the bloody time. They don't care. They just want to go around being cynical because they're journalists. ... No. He didn't have a chance with them really.

Marc Bolan, as told to Anne Nightingale:
The initial idea was a simple one; a documentary type coverage of the Wembley concert, with these parts depicting different aspects of my life. The idea grew until the final film became almost surrealistic. And so the whole thing came together and it was a groove. Elton played with us for hours and we did lots of Rock 'n' Roll. In the end we had hours and hours of film. We did some filming at Lennon's place where I did a medley of hits with a

string quartet. Everyone's eating cream cakes and Mickey's a vampire and there's strawberry jam dripping down his chin ... disgusting! But basically it's just Rock 'n' Roll. All the hits like GET IT ON are there, the film represents the T. Rex thing really. That's nice because you forget it so quickly. When I see the film, it's like seeing something that happened twenty years ago. The way it was put together was very loose. It does look like it was worked out, but really it wasn't. We had fun making it and I'm happy with it. Really happy.

Tony Visconti:
He wouldn't have lasted five minutes on a film set if he had a really powerful director.

Steve Currie:
Marc was an individual, Marc would never have played on anyone else's band; this shows right the way through his career, from the period of John's Children to the formation of T. Rex. It all was a transitional period of him working out how he was going to do it, but he could never have played in anyone else's band.

Tony Visconti:
He tried to manipulate people in the media, for instance, the cover of the SLIDER album; it's an album that's got

Above. Marc, Eric Hall and Gloria Jones. Below left, Elton John and Marc.

the picture of him wearing a top hat on the cover. . . . Well, I took that picture. I remember distinctly, we took that when we were filming *Born to Boogie* and Ringo was busy with his Arrowflex 35 mm camera. Ringo was busy being director and all that. I played the part of the conductor of the orchestra. Marc was a photographer and he handed me his Nikon camera and he said: "Take a few shots of me." He posed, like he put his top hat on and I ran off a whole roll of film. A few weeks later, at his flat, he showed me the contact prints and I said, "Oh, great, I took that picture, I took that piece", and Marc said, "Great, circle the ones you took, initial them and if I use them on the album, I'll give you a credit for it." And lo and behold, it was the front and back cover. It said, "Photo taken by Ringo Starr" in big letters, which really pissed me off.

Eric Hall:
He always made sure he knew the right people.

Steve Currie:
The most embarrassing thing I saw, was Elton's birthday party. Marc sent a big thing with his Wembley concert on it; to Elton, as a card. It was like saying: "Wish you were here and I'm the greatest." He had it sent down in an Avis truck with the roadie, which wasn't very friendly.... It ended up in the swimming pool anyway.

Gloria Jones:
We were in Paris; this was around '74, some time around there. And he flew everyone in from the Press; flew them over from England to Paris, just so he'd be able to do interviews and that, so the children there in England—you know, his fans and everyone—could know what he was doing.

Tony Visconti:
He always reckoned that you had to tell people that you were successful, otherwise they wouldn't take any notice of you. He would justify his lying by saying: "I'm just being professional." I remember that he was always making a film with David Niven; and that was a total lie. David Niven never acknowledged the fact that he was making a film with Marc Bolan. But Marc, if you pressed him about it, would say: 'Well look, I'm not making a film. I'm just being professional. You have to say these things." That's where he didn't have to overplay himself. He had it; he

had all the charisma, all the stuff going for him. He didn't have to go that far. But he did.

Steve Currie:
There was a funny incident at Orly Airport. Marc was buying some tickets and there was this guy in front of him, and Marc was saying: "I'm Marc Bolan. Give us some elbow room." And this guy wasn't giving an inch. Marc always had this ambition to have a gold American Express Card. This guy in front of us pays for his ticket with just that; a gold American Express Card. That ruined his day.

Eric Hall:
Marc was a terrible name dropper, even in those days; a monster name dropper. I tell you, he'd ring me up and say to me: "What are you doing for Sunday lunch?" I'd say: "Sorry I'm busy." Marc would say: "What a shame, because I've got David Bowie, David Niven, Frank Sinatra, the King of Siam even, all coming round for lunch. Pity..." Mind you, you could never be sure. Maybe if I'd gone round for Sunday lunch, I might well have met Frank Sinatra, the King of Siam and all the rest of them. That's the way he was.

Steve Currie:
I used to confront him with the truth and if he continued lying, either I would get up and walk away, or I'd just tell

Below, T. Rex in concert.

him: "You don't have to tell me." He couldn't hide the truth from the members of the band because we knew the truth.

Tony Visconti:
Marc had this one quirk in his nature where he had to always lie, you know?.

> I've constructed your frame
> In a plasticine game
> And your eyes are the sweets of my youth
> But I'm naked and bare
> In the ice of your stare
> And I'm useless at telling the truth...
> From JUNIPER SUCTION by Marc Bolan

Steve Harley:
He was slightly pathological. You can't call it lying. He didn't lie. But he lived in a fantasy world about himself. He had this incredible overactive imagination that, sometimes, after a couple of drinks, it lost touch with reality. His imagination started to take over. It was almost schizophrenic. If he'd start fantasising at me I'd say: "Look, don't give me this bullshit. Don't lay it on me, lay it on other people, 'cos I know you better, I know the truth, so don't talk to me like that." It was all good banter; I mean he could take that from people that he loved. He could take them standing up. People would say: "Hey, Marc, slow down and stop this. Let's get to the truth now." He could take this, he didn't mind. Sometimes he got very hurt for a few minutes 'cos he'd been found out. He was continually getting caught smoking round the back of the toilets at school, you know what I mean? He didn't mind.... Just look hurt sometimes.

Steve Harley and Marc.

Eric Hall:
He'd say to me, I've got this exhibition in Paris next week and I'd say: "Marc, this is Eric you're talking to." He'd give you that funny look and smile at you, you know, and then start talking about something else. Oh, I knew he had flair

for drawing. I know that. It just didn't turn me on.... He was a very sensitive lad though.

> Just because Toulouse Lautrec
> Painted some chick in the rude
> Doesn't give you the right
> To steal my night
> And leave me naked in the nude
> From DESDEMONA by Marc Bolan

Steve Turner, *Beat Instrumental*:
... Marc explained to me that his biggest influences of the year were Chuck Berry and Alphonse Mucha. And before you ask your local record shop for the latest Mucha album I must point out that he is in fact a painter! Marc showed me some of his work in a huge art book he took from his shelves. He also explained to me how much effect architecture could have on a person's response to the music they hear in a certain room.

Steve Harley:
"Hey!" he'd say, "I'm doing a movie, a three million dollar movie. Jack Nicholson's going to be the star, I'm producing it, I'm going to be in it and – er – you're going to co-star."
"Oh yeah? What's it about?"
"I've just finished the script."
"What is the script?"
He'd stand up and pace around my living room, from one end to the other, pausing now and again to lean on something. Then he'd purse his lips and go:
"There's these two guys. One of them gets a lucky break at the gambling tables. The other one..."
And I'd say, "Yeah yeah?" Then he'd pace backwards, up to the other end of the room. All eyes would be on him, everyone in the room would be transfixed by his madness. And the fact was, everyone knew he was putting us on. It could be hilariously funny. He was brilliantly inventive. I mean, he could create a scenario off the top of his head. And if you didn't like one, there'd be another. The only person who didn't know he was putting us on, was Marc. Even when you told him, he still wouldn't believe it. But I loved him for it.

B. P. Fallon:
He didn't need an aeroplane to fly.

June Bolan:
He was like a sponge, and I mean that in the best possible way. He wanted to learn, and learn he did. But only the things he was interested in, not the general knowledge sort of thing, nothing like that. But he was extraordinarily well read. And he wrote totally phonetically; he had no idea of spelling.... He learned from people. He took all their best bits, channelled them out after he'd stamped them with his own stamp.

Tony Visconti:
He didn't read much at all. Books had to be read to him.

He ate, drank, slept, lived, talked music and the show business life. Alvin Stardust.

Steve Turner, *Beat Instrumental*:

That's where June was great. She read all the classics to him and she read all of the Lord of the Rings.

Although Marc has been built up into a 'pop star', and all that it entails, he is far from a naive glamour-seeker with a few oddball ideas about an apocalypse. Just to glance through his bookshelves is enough indication of the areas of thought he has studied. Poetry, science fiction, mysticism, horror, magic and Eastern thought are all well represented and one small pile of books contains the life stories of Rock 'greats' such as Elvis, Adam Faith, Tommy Steele and The Beatles.

Tony Visconti:

He listened to music a lot. Many times Marc used to hire sixteen-millimetre films and we used to look at them and have laughs. There was a period when we all bought the new Polaroid camera when it came out and we used to take hundreds of photos of each other. He loved the Rock and Roll life. He really did; he loved it.

Steve Turner, *Beat Instrumental*:

His record selection is also extensive and there must be few artists who are not represented somewhere there. As Marc said, he listens to everything, "...to see what's going down."

Steve Harley:

He was a music freak; he was in love with music, modern Rock. Rock 'n' Roll was his entire life. He'd come in and he'd turn me on to the new black stuff from America. He'd rave about it and we'd talk about how wonderful these guys played and what great productions they were.

Tony Visconti:

He'd buy about fifty records a week, play them all, and then play me a track or two and ask me what I thought of them. I'd say it was nice and he'd say it was rubbish. He'd play Eric Clapton, and he'd say: "What do you think of that, Tony?" and I'd say: "That was a good lick there." And he'd say: "Rubbish!" He'd say that he could play better than that. He had this side to him where he had to — even to me — lie. He just wouldn't admit his level of musicianship.

Steve Harley:

Listen, the man was a poet.

Adrian:

He was the best poet in the world. I got into trouble at school, in English A level. I couldn't be bothered with Wordsworth and that; I just used to keep writing about Marc. And I failed the exam in the end.

Eric Hall:

I've seen his poetry. I'm not into poetry so maybe I'm no judge, but for me, as a member of the public, it was nonsensical; I just didn't know what he was trying to say.

Pages from one of Marc's notebooks.

Marc Bolan, as told to Keith Altham, *Look Now*:
I am a teenage idol I suppose. But I'm not a teenybop idol and I'd be really insulted if the Press wrote me off as anything less than a musician and I regard myself as some kind of poet. At least the sales of my book of poems would suggest a few people seem to think I have something worth reading.

Steve Harley:
I mean, there were lines in DANDY IN THE UNDERWORLD which were just stunning; very sort of fantasy stuff. It's not T. S. Eliot, but at the same time, it was very bizarre Marc Bolan; at his most fantastic. There are some very strange lines in there: 'Prince of Darkness...' but it wasn't a development musically.

Tony Visconti:
There was definitely a touch of genius there, for him to have gone so far; to have made it with such a limited knowledge of music. But I'd say he had a very good knowledge of poetry and what words went nice with other words. Poetically he was very good. Excellent in fact.

> Nijinsky hind
> Is a wisp of our world
> through the heart's eye
> It's horns are white hide
> From the skin of our Lord
> When his youth stood
> Wondrous and fair
> Like a sea.
>
> Nijinsky hind
> Is a remnant of Earth
> As it once stood
> A likeness in flesh
> Of the magic
> Contained in a pearl's shell
> Breathing its breath
> Uniquely.
>
> Nijinsky hind
> Was begotten
> From man's thoughts
> Of kindness
> Its hoofs shod with gold
> Are the textures of Earth's distant future
> Gilded and tall
> Like a hall.
> NIJINSKY HIND by Marc Bolan

Marc was a superb poet all the time. His early lyrics were fabulous, and even his Rock 'n' Roll lyrics are very cheeky and very imaginative.

Marc Bolan, Nov. 1972:
Cars in particular appear in my lyrics, sometimes purely because interesting-looking cars are like works of art; anything is, in the modern-day world. A cup and saucer can be a work of art, if you want. But I just use them because all I keep seeing is cars, all over the place, and people put a lot of status on them sexually. So many things about them just interests me. I don't know how they work either, which fascinates me slightly.

> M-m-m-m-m-m-m-m-m-my Mustang Ford
> My baby she knows I'm on the scene
> My baby keeps asking where I've been
> My baby's guessing that I'm messing
> It's all put together with alligator leather
> My baby she knows I'm no fool
> My baby she says hey keep cool
> My baby don't realise I'm hypnotised
> It's all put together with alligator leather
> M-m-m-m-m-m-m-m-m-my Mustang Ford.
> MUSTANG FORD by Marc Bolan

Steve Harley:
Marc was a real bona fide poet; let no one tell you any different. He was a poet. I've read his poetry book THE WARLOCK OF LOVE of which he was really proud, and also poetry that he wrote up until the end; he was writing all the time. He used to read it to me. He'd stand up in the middle of a room and do his big Laurence Olivier impersonation, reciting Shakespeare or his own poetry.

Marc Bolan, Nov. 1972:
I don't see myself as either a poet or a musician, unless I look in a mirror! I have days when I'm just a guitarist and I play guitar all day and I just don't want to sing. I have some days when I think I'm Caruso and I sing my head off. And there are other days when I just write. This period of my life I'm purely a Rock 'n' Roll star.

B. P. Fallon:
Boley was a communicator and he was good at it.

Gloria Jones:
He loved the business. He loved being a performer.

Tony Visconti:
To have gone so far with such a limited musical knowledge is amazing. I think you can only attribute that to genius.... That's why I stuck it out with him so long.

B. P. Fallon:
I left him in '72. I'd achieved what I wanted to do, which was to tell people about him.

Mickey Finn:
The reason we split was that I wanted to branch out and

... Marc and I used to be very, very, close.

write with my own band. I decided that we'd quit. Marc always had to have his own way and it had just gone on a bit too long. I needed a break.

June Bolan:
I left him at the end of '73. It would have been in the summer of '73.

B. P. Fallon:
We never stopped sort of hanging out and stuff like that, so it wasn't as if I was gone and he was on one planet and I was on another.

Mickey Finn:
I don't know actually if he was upset at us splitting up, but I was certainly upset. It's like we had lived together for six or seven years on the road, and all of a sudden, he's not there. I'd wake up at home and pick up the phone and order room service like I was still on the road and in a hotel somewhere. I was so geared up to that sort of thing.

John Blake, *Evening News,* May 23rd 1973:
We talked about women, and then wives, and then his wife June. "I love June very much," he says. "But people are weird, things change and I never know. But I'm very happy at the moment. Marriage is a great basis for sanity. I'd have opted out years ago without June. There's no doubt about that."

Mick O'Halloran:
Marc rang me down on the phone and said: "Come up. I want to talk to you in my room." I went up to his room and he said that June had left him. I couldn't believe him. Then he sat down and he was crying, just like a baby.

June Bolan:
It was after the SLIDER album; it was at that time when it started. I mean, we were on tour and he became incredibly violent. He was never a violent person really and if he became cross, he used to hit himself on his head. I mean, he never hit me. He usually did it when gigs went bad.

Marc Bolan, as told to David Hancock, *National Rock Star,* Oct. 23rd 1976:
It just suddenly happened one day. Long after June left I did have fits of violence. I still do. It's the poetic side of my nature; kicking television screens and throwing hatchets at pictures of Elvis Presley.

Steve Harley:
Marc was Rock 'n' Roll personified. He was really a star and he had the pose off pat. In fact, he almost created it. He had the Elvis pose, the Elvis movements and the Elvis star attitude.

June Bolan, as told to Danae Brook, *Evening News*:
He was a totally immediate person. That's why I could never deny his presence. He lived in the moment. He was always aware of himself.

B. P. Fallon:
He was always conscious about his audience because he was very conscious about himself.

Steve Harley:
If Marc wasn't in the spotlight, he'd sit in the corner and just wouldn't talk until things had quietened down and then he would leap in and snatch that spotlight back. In any room, in any party, any club, he'd be continually looking for where that spotlight was and moving towards it.

B. P. Fallon:
Boley would have made his mark, whenever he spent time here.

Steve Harley:
Ceaselessly, the man was a star. He couldn't believe he could be anything else.

Tony Visconti:
This was his main internal struggle, I think. There were times I would sit up with him all night, just doing a fifteen-second guitar solo; there were times he wanted to be a musician, and there were times he just simply wanted to be a star.

B. P. Fallon:
He could have been a painter; he could have been a sculptor. He was a brilliant man who made use of Rock 'n' Roll because that was the media for him, this time around.

Steve Harley:
It was beyond his grasp to accept that he was just a geezer, a mere mortal. He might even stand up and chin you if you said that to him.

Tony Visconti:
This was his conflict. It was always inside him. I could capture his creative moments; I could capture him on tape when he really wanted to be an artist. Unfortunately, most of the time, he wanted to be a star.

Steve Harley:
It would be heresy to say to Marc Bolan: You're not a star at all; you're just an ordinary cat who makes records, who writes songs. That would be sacrilegious!

David Neill, *Record Weekly,* Jan. 1st 1972:
It was nightcap time in a plushy hotel bar. Fifty soberly-minded commercial travellers who had been at a sales conference were drinking their gin. For a minute or two they did not notice the slight, frizzy-haired figure wearing green women's shoes and a torn fur coat. When they did silence fell until four men shouted: "Get her!"
The fur-coated figure drew himself up to his full height of just over five feet and announced: "It is quite possible that in a year's time I will have fifty men like you working for me. I've got a Rolls-Royce outside. If you saw me get out of it, you would respect me. You ought to think of that before being offensive."
The salesmen learned that 'she' was, in fact, Marc Bolan of the T. Rex Rock group. No doubt, to them, it was a unique experience.

Tony Visconti:
He had a definite effect on British music, from RIDE A WHITE SWAN to GET IT ON to TELEGRAM SAM. I mean music was going in a dangerous direction; getting too serious for itself.

John Blake, *Evening News,* May 23rd 1973:
T. Rex, the most sought-after band since the Monkees, is finished in its present form: "At the moment we are not playing live anywhere at all." He told me, when we met in a Soho pub.
He arrived at the pub wearing a £50 feather boa from Harrods and carrying a silver cane. No one appeared to recognise him.

Steve Currie:
The glamour, the clothes, stuff like that, that was forced on us by Marc. There used to be a saying: Anyone caught wearing a tee shirt would be shot at dawn.

B. P. Fallon:
It's the male that struts; that element had been denied and Bolan put that straight.

Steve Currie:
We used to 'lose' suitcases on the road. We were all sent down to Granny Takes A Trip boutique, and the Alkasura boutique in the King's Road, but we 'lost' all those clothes

... It's the male that struts.

in one suitcase. A couple of quid to the porter — lose these, sort of thing.

Gloria Jones:
When I first worked for Marc, we had two other singers and one of the girls, she decided she was going to wear a platinum wig on stage. And I mean, how can you do that with Mister Bolan? I'll never forget it; he was so funny. We went into the dressing room and Marc was like: Wow! What is this? You know, we had got the girl to look really psychedelic. Marc was really great. He came up to her and he said: "Honey, I don't care how many wigs you have on. You can never upstage Bolan." We all just fell about laughing.

Mick O'Halloran:
Of course he wore very unorthodox clothes; not the sort of clothes that anybody would normally wear.

B. P. Fallon:
He was always that little step ahead.

Alvin Stardust:
He would never have stopped. He would always have gone forward.

Tony Visconti:
Marc actually used to dress up for sessions, as if the sessions were gigs. He would put on a show for everyone present, including the engineers, the tea boys, it didn't matter; Marc Bolan was a star in the studio.

Steve Currie:
I remember doing some sessions with Donovan in Munich. Marc was semi producing, semi advising; he was out in the studio every two minutes, telling Donovan what to play and how to play it.

Tony Visconti:
Musically he revived Rock 'n' Roll; he brought it back in a new form. The Press termed it 'Glam Rock'.

Steve Currie:
As far as guitaring goes, Marc was a funny guitarist. He just had that tremendous energy that if it wasn't done his way, it wasn't done at all.

Tony Visconti:
He made it possible for David Bowie to become successful. There was a brief period where he did actually revolutionise. Image wise, he made Rock 'n' Roll respectable by being outrageous; this, indeed, was a credit to him.

Steve Harley:
I'll tell you one thing he was; apart from being a born

Gloria Jones

fantasiser, he was extremely — to the point of embarrassment — extremely generous.

Steve Currie:
He was generous in every way.

Tony Visconti:
He used to say things like: "If GET IT ON makes the top ten in the States, I'll buy you a Harley Davidson Electroglide." It did make the top ten several months later; the motorbike never materialised. He was always promising us all motorbikes; he was trying to do the Elvis image.

Steve Currie:
He bought me a gold watch. And at least half a dozen guitars.

Robin Nash

Steve Harley:
I've go so many things he gave me of his own possessions. He'd just walk in and give me books, or records that were irreplaceable; bring in copies that I knew he couldn't replace. But he'd scribble all over it in some unintelligible hieroglyphics and insist it was for me.

Steve Currie:
We had a few words on one American tour and next morning there was this knock at the door from the roadie and there were two guitars, as a make-up present.

Steve Harley:
He had no love for material things at all, and although he treasured certain possessions, he would give them away as a token of his love. On one occasion I had admired a beautiful leather-bound volume of Shakespeare's complete works that Marc had in his home. The following week Marc brought it to me as a present, and he had scribbled on the fly leaf: "From a modern bard to a Cockney Rebel, whom I love, Marc."

June Bolan:
He was a great guy. You see, he wasn't like people. It all sounds so awful, especially now he's dead, but he wasn't like people.

Tony Visconti:
There are very few people you meet in life who are born leaders. He had that quality. If he wasn't a singer or a Rock star, he could have been a politician.

Robin Nash:
BBC TV Producer, Top Of The Pops
Marc had that wonderful charismatic quality, but you can't define it.

Tony Visconti:
He was very charismatic, he was very good looking and he knew exactly what he wanted and he was unashamed as to how to get it.

David Neill, *Record Weekly,* Jan. 1st 1972:
T. Rex's managers have to work out elaborate manoeuvres to get the group off stage unscathed... and even more elaborate ones to get them away from the theatre. Even ambulances and police Black Marias have been used.

Tony Visconti:
People would often curse him behind his back, but they would respect him and do what he said. And enjoy being part of the set-up. But sometimes he did go over the top.

Steve Currie:
I had a tremendous protectional thing for him; I had a punch-up in Air London one night.

B. P. Fallon:
We never ever had an argument.

Tony Visconti:
He was very powerful, very magnetic. I've seen him in fits of rage, shouting at geezers twice his size; I mean, he couldn't possibly have defended himself against them. But they'd be trembling in his presence because he was powerful; he was a very, very strong person; very strong-willed.

Steve Currie:
He blacked my eye but I split his lip, which really was over a very silly thing. But then again, he was drunk. Unfortunately, he began believing in his own lies, like the eighteen Rolls-Royces and the thirty-six yachts.

John Blake, *Evening News*:
...he said that the strain of constant tours was beginning to affect his mind. "Mentally it would have killed me. The whole strain in your head warps your mind. I'm still not sure of my sanity half the time, seriously. There are a million things that contribute. The pressure is fantastic. I'm a million-pound industry but I'm only a kid really."

Tony Visconti:
His first manager, Peter Jenner, described him aptly I think: A flower child with a knife up his sleeve.

Danae Brook, *Evening News*:
The peak of his career came in 1971, but that was the

place from which he fell, locking out his friends who were part of his creative ascent; constantly paranoid, buying people with money and then finding they would never give him the things which love and shared experience had. "He lost touch with reality," says June now. "He was dazzled by his own myth."

Steve Currie:
Marc was never a producer. He had a megalomania about every instrument. You couldn't discipline him to the basic bass, drums and a slight amount of keyboards. The day Marc first heard of the synthesiser, it was thirty thousand string machines! That lost him his simple, almost naive, way of writing. He wanted to be another Rick Wakeman through somebody else, but Marc's writing was very naive straight Rock 'n' Roll. I think that was the beginning of his downfall.

Tony Visconti:
I tried to disbelieve what the Press was saying about everything sounding the same from Marc Bolan. I tried to say No.

Marc Bolan, as told to David Neill, *Record Weekly*:
I'm not an arrogant person. The only time I get arrogant is when I am not getting service because people think I'm a freak. You just have to let them know that you've got the money and are prepared to spend it.

Tony Visconti:
He used to hate to spend money!

Mick O'Halloran:
When he started having hit records, he started worrying about money.

Tony Visconti:
With his tax situation the albums had to be done overseas, and whereas Bowie would go and hire a chateau in France for a month, bringing his own chef and all that, Bolan would hire it for three days and have us working flat out, virtually seventy-two hours.

Mick O'Halloran:
But at the period of time that I was first with Marc, he never worried about money. We didn't care, just as long as I had a bit of float just to get petrol, to get to the gig, wherever we were going.

Steve Currie:
The SLIDER was done in twenty-seven and a half hours. I've still got the invoice.

Tony Visconti:
It was around this period I said: "This guy's making all

sorts of money. Why do we have to rush through things like this?" And that's when I got a bit disenchanted. I stopped being a fan.

Steve Currie:
My favourite was ELECTRIC WARRIOR. There was a lot of Tony Visconti influence on that.

Tony Visconti:
We were turning into a factory, you know? It was done so quickly. We were just adding our usual echoes to make it sound like T. Rex. There was a formula that I had set up over the years; you know, you put a type of echo on the drums, a type of echo on Marc's voice, a kind of phasing on the guitars and then you put the whole lot through a compressor. It was a thing, and it was being done so quickly. Look, we were arriving at a final mix in half an hour, whereas it used to take several hours or half a day! Marc turned to me and smiled and said: "Cheap, isn't it?" He acknowledged the fact that we had it down to an absolute science, an absolute formula. I used to do T. Rex sessions like you could wake me up in the middle of the night, you know; like, put me behind a desk I knew exactly what to do.

Steve Currie:
I think if the Bolan/Visconti partnership had carried on, it could have been another Lennon/McCartney; Visconti's musical knowledge and Marc's knack of writing.

Tony Visconti:
It all got a bit frustrating. We parted our ways. I just handed in my notice.

Tony Visconti

Steve Currie:
Once Marc started to do it himself, that's when I began to lose interest.

Tony Visconti:
The band resented the fact that we were doing these songs so quickly. I mean, I would just get my drum sound together, I might not even have the tom-tom mike turned on yet, and Marc would rush back in for a playback and say: "I like that. That's a take." And the drummer, Bill, would be cursing. He'd say: "I didn't even know the bloody song yet!" Marc would just say: "Don't worry. That'll be good. I'll put about five or six guitars on it." A lot of things were done in a shoddy way and the band resented him for that.

Steve Currie:
It lost the magic for me.

Gloria Jones:
Musically Marc was always aware of his direction. Marc was his own creator of his music.

A doodle on words from Marc's notebook.

Tony Visconti:
There was the time Marc tried to produce. He went through this period where he resented me, you know; that I was doing so much for the T. Rex sound. After a while I was playing bass on a few of the records, and after Flo and Eddy wouldn't do the backing vocals for him anymore, I was doing the backing vocals. On TELEGRAM SAM that's me, singing up very high there; and I was doing the string arrangements. I was as much the T. Rex sound as Marc was. I mean, he wrote the songs, played the guitar and sang. But all the rest was the band and myself.

Steve Harley:
Marc never saw it. He'd never learn that the best thing was not to be autonomous but to go to someone else, a second pair of ears, detached and objective about what you were doing.

Tony Visconti:
I believed in him. And I always believed he would have progressed too. I figured he'd grow. I was always aware of

his six or seven chords but I figured it was only a matter of a few months, you know, he's going to learn a few more chords. He might take six months off, a year; he might come up with something really fantastic.

> One day we change from children into people
> One day we change . . .
> From SEAGULL WOMAN by Marc Bolan

He never did, that's why I split with him. I'd say from TELEGRAM SAM onwards he just stayed down; I think from TELEGRAM SAM on it just became a formula. We just got stuck there. I stayed on until the single TRUCK ON and to me that was the ultimate.

> If I could have grown
> All upon my own
> If I could have grown
> I grew
> If I could have grew
> I do
> If I had a throne
> You could call it home
> If I cry
> My tears are yours
> To open any frozen doors
> Hey, let's do it like we're friends
> Let's do it do it
> Hey, let's do it like we're friends.
> DIAMOND MEADOWS by Marc Bolan

He could be as rough as could be, sometimes, you know; really make us all feel awful. But, it was really worth while, for the period. . . . Shame.

Steve Currie:
I used to be shop steward; we used to pull strikes. At a certain point I would withdraw the labour of the band; I'd say we're not going to go on until certain demands are met. The early days, we all went the same class. But one particular time I was doing an Atlantic flight to LA; it was Tony Howard (Marc's manager) and Marc up in the front. Tony Howard came back and went "Moo-moo" to us like we were a load of cattle. That was it. When we got off the plane, we weren't playing. And so we hung out and got first-class seats. But they were management problems. They weren't anything to do with Marc.

June Bolan:
America wasn't good for him; it destroyed him.

Mick O'Halloran:
That was his one ambition in life, to try and make the States; break the States record-wise, you know. Really know that you'd been over there.

Davey Lutton, Steve Currie and Mickey Finn.

Tony Visconti:
Well, he had absolutely no effect on the States.

June Bolan:
He wanted America. It became obsessive. It got all out of context. I think he thought, because it happened here as he planned it, he thought America would go like that; it would pick up on the English, German and Japanese thing.

Steve Currie:
On the American tour he gave us a forty-five-minute lecture. He went into telling us how we weren't good enough and that he could replace us in thirty seconds.

I'm the King of the highway
I'm the Queen of the hop
You should see me
At the Governor's ball
Doing the rip-off bop

I'm a social person
I'm the creature in disguise
There's a man with a whip
On his silver lip
Living inside my eyes.

From RIP-OFF by Marc Bolan

June Bolan:
He did an amazing tour in Japan and I think he thought it would automatically follow. But, of course, it didn't, because America is very different. In America they are more demanding; they demand a higher standard of professionalism; and because he spanned the 'teenybop' and hippy thing here. In America they don't have that sort of thing. America is very cut and dried as to which category, or which audience one appeals to basically.

Marc Bolan, Nov. 1972:
There's only people. You can't 'audience' people. I still get letters from forty-five-year-old dons, talking about things

America 1973, with Gloria, in the back seat of a limousine.

like great scripts; about what METAL GURU was all about — and that sold eight million.

Steve Currie:
There's that well-known story outside one of the big New York hotels on whatever avenue. David, the drummer, was last out of the hotel; we were all crammed in the car with hand luggage and Marc and Gloria were in the other car. So, Marc got out of the car and realised that everybody was crammed tight. There was just room in my car for somebody else, so as Marc opened the door, David, being the last out, was physically hurtled onto the street. And his luggage came out after him, so Marc slammed the door and locked it. But that was a time when he was drinking very heavily.

Gloria Jones:
Marc didn't have a drinking problem; I mean, he had gone through quite a bit before he and I were together.

June Bolan:
He was drinking quite heavily at this time.

Gloria Jones:
All of that with Marc was showbiz.

Steve Currie:
He used to drink vodka and wine. I've seen him go through sixteen bottles of Rosé during the two o'clock session, till sort of four or five in the morning. He couldn't really cope with it. He'd wake up the next morning forgetting what he'd done in the studio.

> Meeting behind the iron sling
> My brandy tongue was like a caterpillar thing
> From THE SCENES OF DYNASTY
> by Marc Bolan

There used to be cans and cans of unused tape, and once he got through that drunken stage into sheer alcoholic megalomania, he'd just say to the studio: "I've got a great idea for a song." And we all had to work it out as fast as we could. Then he'd wipe out the guitars and just use the bass and drum tracks and build over it. . . . That's not the way to write a song.

June Bolan:
He was drinking on the last tour I did with him in America. He met Gloria.

Gloria Jones:
I met him in 1972.

B. P. Fallon:
I think Gloria's a wondrous singer.

June Bolan:
We employed her as a session singer—a back-up singer. She did one tour with two other chicks.

Gloria Jones:
I received a telephone call from Marc's manager, Tony Howard; they were in Houston, Texas. He asked me if I could get two girls.

June Bolan:
Gloria's not a good lead singer but she's a very good musician; a good record producer.

Gloria Jones:
We arrived there, at the Continental High House, and his valet opened the door for us and had us come in and sit down. He went out and ordered some tea and so finally, about ten minutes later, Marc came from the bedroom into the living room, and—oh he looked gorgeous!

June Bolan:
They did the tour, and on that tour he started to go very peculiar, because the tour wasn't going well.

> There was a time when everything was fine
> You got drunk all day like it was wine
> And all the children
> They put flowers in their hair
> And all grown ups
> They put daggers there instead.
> From RAW RAMP by Marc Bolan

He had lost his direction.

Steve Currie:
I found him wandering the corridors at about three o'clock one morning in this Munich hotel; I'd come in from a night club. He was standing there, in tears because he could feel the vibes of all the people that had been massacred by the Nazis in the Second World War.

B. P. Fallon:
He had a knowledge about things that weren't logically explainable.

Steve Currie:
I took him back to his room and made him coffee all night.

June Bolan:
He always believed when I left him, I had abandoned him.

And he never forgave me.

> It was grand to have known her
> It was grand to have grown her
> I don't need anyone
> To dictate all my fun
> Smile your smile and then run.
> From SCENESCOF by Marc Bolan

I left him because of Gloria.

Gloria Jones:
He didn't approach me for one whole year. And then, when we did decide we should be together, it was really a beautiful decision. It was never anything nasty.

Gloria Jones, Milwaukee 1973.

June Bolan:
I couldn't cope with that anymore. I'd done it too many times; I knew I'd die if I stayed. I know that sounds very Sarah Bernhardt, but I knew I just had to leave.

Gloria Jones:
No matter how people try and make it look, I never broke up any home.

June Bolan:
He wasn't like people; it's a very hard thing to maintain any relationship, because he wasn't like people. Usually

one learns things from one relationship that holds one in good stead for the next. And so it goes on through life; I mean, that's the normal pattern of life. But it doesn't hold you in good stead. It really fucks you up, because he wasn' people. I'm not saying he was super-human or super-psychic; he was just very special and I can't find the words

Shallow are the actions
Of the children of men
Fogged was their vision
Since the ages began
And lost like a lion
In the canyons of smoke
Girl it's no joke.
From MONOLITH by Marc Bolan

He was really a full-time person, twenty-four hours a day And there was no way you could get out of it.

Marc Bolan, as told to Jan Iles, *Record Mirror*:
I recently split with my wife. It wasn't very harassing. mean, do I look heartbroken?

June Bolan:
It's a case of one's life being touched by him.

Marc Bolan, as told to Jan Iles, *Record Mirror*:
We just grew apart. We couldn't relate to each other any more.

June Bolan:
I don't know what good husbands are, I just knew Marc

Marc Bolan, as told to Jan Iles, *Record Mirror*:
I was away most of the time. I guess it's very hard being the wife of a Rock star, 'cos you live in the shadow of someone else and, well, I'm a lunatic anyway; all artistic people are.

I could have loved you girl
Like a planet
I could have chained your heart
To a star
But it really doesn't matter at all
But it really doesn't matter at all
Life's a gas, I hope it's gonna last.
From LIFE'S A GAS by Marc Bolan

June Bolan:
In the end I came to feel that I had nothing more to give him; I was drained; I was absolutely used up.

Mick O'Halloran:
I never dreamed that he and June would ever part. They seemed so much in love with each other.

Marc Bolan, as told to David Hancock, *National Rock Star,* Oct. 1976:
The reason we got married was because it was a fun thing at the time. Now it seems a dumb thing to have done. The facts are that she left me and we just grew apart.

June Bolan, as told to Danae Brook, *Evening News*:
You see, it was the third time he'd had an affair. He couldn't just go off and have a quick scene. He had to fall in love. I'd been through it twice already; once it was another singer, once a painter, and I knew the signs.

Mick O'Halloran:
I never dreamed that could happen. I think that then started the bad omens; whatever was happening, something bad started to happen.

June Bolan, as told to Danae Brook, *Evening News*:
I knew what he was like when he was in love because it was just like we used to be. When I found out about Gloria I just couldn't take it again. It was too painful.

Marc Bolan, as told to David Hancock:
Three years is sufficient time to become bored with people. At this point in time (Oct. 1976) Gloria doesn't want to get married, and neither do I. This old line about 'for the baby's sake' is bull.

Adrian:
Gloria once gave me a lift in her car, from Birmingham back to London. It was after a gig. She straightened him out a lot.

Gloria Jones:
I didn't sort out Marc musically. I was in Marc's life as far as giving him certain things that he's never had before.

B. P. Fallon:
She's more close to Marc in a way, though June is too; in her make-up, in a loony sense. Gloria's very strong too, but in a different way to June.

Marc Bolan, as told to David Hancock:
Looking back I entered into marriage with June too lightly. I was not in control in those days. I was being worked like a work-horse; constantly touring.

Mick O'Halloran:
There was a lot of pressure on him.

Marc Bolan, as told to David Hancock:
Fortunately, later on you can pick and choose, as you can with partners. Actually, there were no great scenes; no smashing things up.

Tony Visconti:
After those years, I consider it was a steady decline from then on. I said goodbye after TRUCK ON.

> So I hide with my head
> In the tent of the bed
> And my body is sucked through your eyes
> Then I quiver and shiver
> And start to deliver
> The goods
> Then I vanish in size.
> From JUNIPER SUCTION by Marc Bolan

Steve Currie:
There was one particular person, close to him, who was bad for him. He created the Marc we all loved to hate; he turned Marc into a machine. He put the germ into Marc's head that he was the greatest thing since sliced bread.

Tony Visconti:
He went down a bit in every way. It's because he took on self-management and took on this responsibility, which he needn't have done. He didn't have to do it. Shame. Pity.

Gloria Jones:
He did build his own career.

Eric Hall:
He'd have his fingers into everything. I mean, if he wanted to go on tour, he would sit down and negotiate with the agent himself, fees, percentages, whatever. It wasn't that he didn't trust anybody. He just loved the business. And a terrible worrier. But this is what made him a professional.

Mick O'Halloran:
What I could never understand is, he didn't need to do that, because he didn't have to worry about anything really. He never worried about money before, but all of a sudden this new Dr Jekyll — or Mr Hyde, I should say — was coming into the man.

Steve Currie:
I didn't get a percentage on the records. I got a wage and a percentage bonus on every gig. It wasn't that much really.

Tony Visconti:
Marc was signed with David Platz up till GET IT ON. I was making what you'd call a normal producer's percentage at that time. I was on the average normal two per cent deal, where my commission was two per cent of the retail price. David Platz was paying me a retainer of twenty-five quid a week, which since we got into the hit situation, he didn't have to pay me that anymore.

Steve Currie:
When I started with the band, it was thirty pounds a week; when I left it was from eighty to a hundred pounds a week, and fifty quid a gig plus double rates for sessions.

Steve Currie, Davey Lutton, Gloria Jones, Marc and Dino Dines at Scorpio Studios; the last photograph taken of T. Rex.

Tony Visconti:
When Marc's contract ran out with David Platz and he didn't resign, I got this ugly letter from Marc's solicitor one day saying that at this phase in Marc's career he felt that he didn't have to pay the producer a percentage any longer and that I should work for a flat fee. The T. Rex thing was growing and growing and I was one of the direct contributors to this phenomenon, so I just phoned him up and said what the hell was this letter all about? For a whole year, after Marc left David Platz, I had worked with the understanding that my royalty of two percent would continue, and then all of a sudden I get this letter. I said to June that Marc wouldn't speak to me; he was too embarrassed by it all. I know you get these solicitors who put ideas into your head so I'm not going to put all the blame on Marc. But he was too embarrassed to talk to me about it, so June said: "Why don't you have lunch with the solicitor?" — which is what I did. The solicitor tried to play my part — my contribution to T. Rex — down. He said: "What exactly is a record producer? What do you do? Just twiddle a few knobs? I mean, Marc is a creative genius." And all that. I said: "Look, you put Marc in a studio and see what you get." I said: "Marc doesn't have a clue what knob does what." I said that I did lots of things but here was I, with all these hits under my belt, hits that I produced, and here was I defending myself to this rotten solicitor — who shall remain nameless! I went back to June and I said: "Look, I can't have any of this. I'll probably quit the situation if you don't come up with the two per cent you promised me a year ago." Marc still wouldn't talk to me, so June came round to the house. She was all tearful and crying and saying how she'd heard about the meeting and how sorry she was. So I got back on to a percentage — but one per cent!

Steve Currie:
I didn't make a fortune, but I enjoyed it. Anyway, what price can you put on job satisfaction?

Mick O'Halloran:
He said: "How much are you getting working for Love Affair?" So I told him. At that time it was £25 a week. So he said: "Well, I'll give you twenty, and if you're any good we'll put your money up." So I said okay and he said: "If we grow, you'll grow" — which I thought was fair enough.

Steve Currie:
I knew I could have earnt more but I've got a nice flat, a car, a motorbike and a horse. I really can't be bothered with meetings at one o'clock in the morning to sort out my supertax. I really enjoyed the music and Marc.

Mick O'Halloran:
He was gradually altering. He wasn't the nice Marc we all knew before, which was so sad, because, before he was so kind and considerate to everybody. Unless you knew him at that time, you just couldn't believe.

Gloria Jones and Marc, Scorpio Studios, during the period when Marc was very much overweight.

Tony Visconti:
I figured, well, if Marc's going to get all shitty on me, it's the beginning of the end. At that time I was just married with a baby on the way; I had my overheads so I accepted those terms; one per cent. I came down.

Mick O'Halloran:
People like John Peel, Bob Harris, various sort of well-known people in this country, knew him, admired and loved him. And all of a sudden they saw the change; I'm sure they did. They started pulling away from the guy. At most concerts that Marc played, there'd always be somebody there; Bob, or John Peel would come along and see him; all sorts of different people. But as soon as he started to change, then they gradually dropped off, and everybody started slagging him. Not their fault. It was perfectly true

Steve Harley, Gloria Jones and Marc.

what they said. Marc couldn't see that the people who he had around him in 1969, or around that period, were the best people for him. They were also friends.

Tony Visconti:
He always insisted he was right and that he knew what he was doing and I think the only thing he finally believed in was record sales. When they finally started to diminish, that was when he finally believed there was something wrong.

Gloria Jones:
I tell you, what happened was, during that time he was having problems staying in the country; he was not very happy about the tax laws round '74. So, what happened was, we did a lot of travelling.

> Ride it on out like a bird in the skyways,
> Ride it on out like you were a bird,
> Fly it all out like an eagle in a sunbeam,
> Ride it all out like you were a bird.
> From RIDE A WHITE SWAN by Marc Bolan

I must tell you, we took the very last voyage on the SS *France*. I'll never forget it, because it was most exciting. I remember, we were there, in the middle of the ocean and Marc had nothing but credit cards. He wanted to see if he could get some money out there, so he wired his assistants. It was amazing. He said: "Hey! Look at me. I'm getting bread in the middle of the Atlantic!"

> Catch a bright star and place it on your forehead,
> say a few spells and there you go.
> Take a black cat, sit it on your shoulder
> And in the morning you'll know all you know.
> From RIDE A WHITE SWAN by Marc Bolan

During that time Marc and I had moved to St John's Wood. We had a beautiful flat there. And it was sad for him, because he always loved it so, you know; he loved England. But then we came to live in Beverly Hills, Benedict Canyon. We had a beautiful home; swimming pool, orange trees, lemon trees, grapefruit trees. But even though we had this beautiful home, still it wasn't London. So during this time he was like, really discouraged, because he wanted to live there. So we went to live in

Gloria Jones with Eric Hall outside London Weekend TV Studios.

Monte Carlo. We had a beautiful flat there that overlooked the Mediterranean and our back balcony overlooked the Swiss Alps. But he worked hard. In fact, what he did, he started creating his new sound, which is very much like the New Evolution type sound that other people are doing in '78. Four, say three years ago, he created that beautiful sound.

Steve Harley:
While he understood how the Rock scene had changed in the last five years, and how people wanted a different type of music, and that there were some incredible players in the world doing these great things, he never ever seemed to work with them. He would still be using guys just to play GET IT ON again, you know, GET IT ON '77 and it always baffled me. I'd say to him so many times, trying as hard as I could not to insult him, but, I'd pick my moment and I'd say: "Look. How come if you know this stuff is so brilliant, how come if you understand this is so good, how come you don't try and develop your own style?" His style of writing combined with a really good producer, that was what he lacked. He needed to be taken into the studio and directed; pushed about.

Tony Visconti:
His musical knowledge wasn't as deep as Elton John's. Marc didn't write chords, so I couldn't go that far with Marc; I had to keep the string arrangements simple.

Alvin Stardust:
There's more to music than just playing; it's character as well. I think character comes out in the sympathy of a song and when Marc was writing something, which was

considered by someone else as a silly bubble-gum or wopbop type of song, or whether they considered it to be one of the most creative young Rock 'n' Roll songs around, it didn't matter. The fact is that Marc's personality and energy came out in his music. And it did.

Eric Hall:
Gloria was a good influence on him.

Gloria Jones:
When I joined the group, T. Rex, let's say, like, we were able to add another dimension to the sound, because I play keyboards. In fact, he had two keyboard players; there was Dino Dines.

Steve Harley:
She looked after him. She controlled his excesses. But she didn't control him like a puppet. She didn't manipulate him; not at all; not in the slightest. Marc was pretty unmanageable, if you want the truth. If you want to know why Marc didn't develop musically—which he didn't—I mean, even down to the last that he and I were writing together, I mean, days before the accident, he was still re-writing GET IT ON. He hadn't moved from GET IT ON and RIDE A WHITE SWAN at all.

Gloria Jones:
Marc, more or less, always had everything that he wanted as far as creative control. As far as I am concerned, I felt that everything he has ever done and everything he did, right up to the time he passed away, was excellent music.

Bob Hart, *The Sun*, Feb. 18th 1977:
Smooth Marc is rocking again....
Beneath the sleek, brilliantined hair, it's still the same Marc Bolan, the man who has seen all the sights in the mad, mad world of pop.
He knows what it's like to struggle for recognition. How it feels to be the hottest Rock star in town. And how much it hurts when you fall from grace.
For the first time Marc feels secure enough to talk about his struggle with drink, drugs and depression. About his enthusiasm for the new Rock energy which as led to the British Punk Rock explosion.
"I consider myself to be an elderly statesman of Punk. The Godfather of Punk, if you like."
"... The Glam Rock thing was all right for the early seventies, but by 1974 I was just bored."
"I got involved with drugs—particularly cocaine. And I started to drink a lot. I just didn't particularly want to be a Rock star any more."

Steve Currie:
Then again, you know what he was like. Anything like alcohol or any kind of stimulant, he was a child; he didn't know when to stop. I get pissed but he'd be lying on the floor, still asking for the syphon to put in his mouth and put down a drop more.... He got very heavily into drugs;

... He was a loyal friend and always totally committed to whatever he was doing.
    Elton John.

From the Granada TV series, MARC.

unfortunately cheap ones, not good quality coke. I don't mind a tipple myself, but the stuff he used to have ... well ...

Bob Hart, *The Sun*:
"But 1977 will be different. With the arrival of the Punks, there is suddenly more energy in the business," continued Marc. "I have stopped using drugs. I stopped drinking six weeks ago. I just want to work."
"... This is going to be my year."

Gloria Jones:
Marc was planning to make me into the number one disc movie star. We used to make these fantastic cassette films of records. That was going to be his next phase; he wanted to get into direction. He'd done film before of course, with Ringo, but he wanted to really get into film much more.

Robin Nash:
In the studio we always got on very well. We never had any problems. Obviously it's a foregone conclusion that Marc was a true professional. He had a job of work to do, he'd come in and do it.

Gloria Jones:
He was a natural performer.

Alvin Stardust:
He ate, drank, slept, lived, talked music and the show-business life.

Tony Visconti:
When things started going bad, he never came back to ask me to work for him because—well, I think it was a matter of intense pride. Also I was working for Bowie again and there was always this vicious competition going on between them. Not on David's side, but Marc was always envious of David.

Bob Hart, *The Sun*, Sept. 10th 1977:
Marc Bolan has pulled off an astonishing television scoop. He has persuaded camera-shy Rock star, David Bowie, to co-host the last show in his weekly pop series, MARC.

Eric Hall:
I remember the time at Granada when David Bowie came all the way over from the States just to appear on Marc's afternoon show. It was Marc's last show of the series and it was a big day for him; I mean, David's a big, big star and to get him to 'schlapp' all the way from America—well, it was quite something.

Tony Visconti:
Marc brought in the 'Glam' thing, but David took it a step

*David Bowie with Marc on the Granada TV series,
MARC.*

further. Marc sort of stayed at one level of dressing up and wore lamé jackets with musical notations on, and things like that. David came out with these beautiful bizarre costumes from Japan, designed by a top Japanese designer. Marc couldn't think on that level. There was always this envy, this jealousy, and the fact I was back with David again put Marc off.

Gloria Jones:
I'll never forget the first time I met him. Blue on his eyes, and he had on a beautiful blue satin shirt, with sleeves that were like wings. Gorgeous.

Steve Currie:
Marc was well ahead of David Bowie.

Tony Visconti:
He gave David Bowie the guitar he used on that last television show.

Bob Hart, *The Sun*:
Bolan told me: "It was David's idea to come on to the programme. He happened to be in town this week and he called me because we are very old friends."

Tony Visconti:
David borrowed Marc's guitar and when Marc died, Marc's people wanted the guitar back.

Eric Hall:
About that time there was some union trouble. I'm not knocking the unions but they had some overtime ban or something and when they wanted to do some backing stuff over, they just pulled the plug out on them. They attacked Muriel (Young) of course, she being the producer. But it wasn't her fault. Nothing she could do. And poor old Marc went to his dressing room and just cried and cried and cried. For hours ...

Muriel Young:
Senior Producer, Granada TV; producer of Marc Bolan's—
TV series, MARC.
I met him first when he was fifteen and never ceased to be amazed at his perception, his vision, his knowledge and his utter commitment to his beloved music.

Bob Hart, *The Sun*:
After Bowie watched a playback of the programme, he told me: "I think it's a great show."
Meanwhile Bolan is negotiating for a new thirteen-part TV series in the New Year.

Granada TV Producer, Muriel Young.

Muriel Young:
... Then to the personal side of Marc. The fun, the poses, the truths, the humour and the heartbreaks, all across him like rainclouds and sun. He felt, he suffered, he laughed and he lived. He wasted not one minute of his days.

> With the morn
> We mount and ride
> Pilgrims of summer
> The swift is our guide.
> From THE PILGRIM'S TALE by Marc Bolan

Alvin Stardust:
He was alive all the time.

B. P. Fallon:
He missed Gloria dreadfully when she was away touring.

Marc and Gloria Jones at a reception.

Steve Harley:
Severely. I mean, I've never seen a man miss a woman so much as he missed Gloria.

Gloria Jones:
We were both searching for something and we found it, because we had so many things in common.

B. P. Fallon:
Their chemistry was fantastic.

Gloria Jones:
It was really funny that first day, 'cos when he came into the room and we were all introducing ourselves, he and I both looked at each other and the contact—the eye contact was really beautiful.

B. P. Fallon:
They were really like a pair of Rock 'n' Roll twins.

> Beneath the bepop moon
> I'm howling like a loon for you
> Beneath the mambo sun
> I've got to be the one for you.
> From MAMBO SUN by Marc Bolan

. . . I sussed and stole a scene from Icarus. . . .

Chris Welch, *Daily Mail*, Sept. 17th, 1977:
Marc Bolan, the pop star who grew from a flower child into a glitter rocker, died in a car crash yesterday....

The Richmond Accident Administration Unit:
The accident occurred at 05:58, September 16th, 1977, and was reported to Barnes Police Station.

Muriel Young:
... I had great affection for him and gratitude too. His advice was always right to the point. He knew the scene backwards, but he was also a seer; he knew the scene forwards too.

Chris Welch, *Daily Mail*:
Few had his grasp of the realities of a hard, tough business. Few could convert fantasies, dreams into facts. ...

Alvin Stardust:
To me, Marc was what the music business, Rock 'n' Roll and entertainment is all about. And that is non-stop. He was always productive, always coming out with something new.

Muriel Young:
... I relied on him a great deal during our TV series together, and I still cannot believe that we will never make the sequel we were planning when he died.

Gloria Jones:
He was such a very intelligent man.

Chris Welch, *Daily Mail*:
His ideas always outstripped his capacity as a song writer, as a lyricist, as a guitarist. But he understood pop music more than most of his critics, or his contemporaries....

Eric Hall:
I saw him the night before he died. We were at Morton's restaurant, Gloria, Gloria's brother Richard, and Marc. I left them about one o'clock. It was a great evening.

Jennifer Sharp:
Club Secretary, Morton's
Marc came in about 12.15 and was quite funny. In actual fact, he'd actually been to see a friend of mine, but because of the late hour, he'd had to throw them out; he was working early the next day. But Marc, Gloria and her brother thought; Twelve o'clock. Must go somewhere. And so they came here, as a nice quiet ending to a nice evening. After having something to eat they came down to the bar. They'd taken quite a fancy to the girl who was playing the piano upstairs in the restaurant, I remember, and they were really very keen about her; in fact, Richard was even talking about how maybe he was going to promote her.
It was a good musical night in the bar that night. Russ

Jennifer Sharp.

was playing the piano; he'd got a bassist there, a guy playing saxophone and somebody else on trumpet. A tremendous musical atmosphere was being generated and Marc and Gloria were getting quite high on it; you know, it was like one of those old-fashioned jam sessions, where all sorts of talented people get up and play for no reason apart from their own pleasure. I suppose the next two hours were just spent with everybody enjoying the music, and chatting, relaxing and just winding down. Then Gloria started to play, with a great deal of reluctance at first, but Marc encouraged her, wanting very much for them all to hear her. She played very beautifully and she sang very beautifully. She just sang love songs for him for about three-quarters of an hour. It was very sweet. It was the early hours in the morning; there were about eight or nine of us all together and quite honestly, we were just spell-bound. To see somebody like Marc, who was a star by everybody's account, and Gloria, who is a very successful record producer and artist in her own right, it was very touching; it all boils down to the fact, that these were two people who were in love with each other, using their talents and music as a means of communicating their affection for each other. And it was touching on both a human level and on a professional level. It made the ordinary ways of saying 'I love you' very paltry by comparison.
I don't know what time everybody left. I think it was about 3.30 a.m. or something, because we were all just going home and everybody said goodnight. They were going to have a barbecue, I remember, and we were all going to go and it was all going to be great fun. And then they just drove off home.

Chris Welch, *Daily Mail*:
The curly-haired singer of T. Rex was killed instantly when a purple Mini GT, driven by his American girl friend, Gloria Jones, smashed into a tree on Barnes Common, not far from his home. He was just 29.

Marc's mother, Mrs Feld, with Rolan, here aged two.

Marc and Gloria Jones in the Mini.

June Bolan:
I heard of his death on the 7.30 news. I woke up early that morning, I don't know why. I switched on my radio by my bed and caught the tail end of the news. It sounded something like '. . . Bolan died in car crash . . .' I opened my eyes and at that moment the telephone rang. It was Ronnie Money; she said it was true. I just said that I couldn't speak now and put the phone down. My immediate thoughts were for his parents; all I thought about was his mother. It was his mother who always idolised him.

Steve Currie:
I had a phone call at 8.30 a.m. from Chris Adamson, a roadie. I've known him for years. He was up early and heard the early news. I got a phone call from the office. . . . Just couldn't believe it. . . . It's very difficult when someone rings you up like that.

Tony Visconti:
My first reaction was shock, like anybody else.

B. P. Fallon:
I was totally freaked out when I heard he had died.

Tony Visconti:
I was asked by the Press to make a statement, but I was absolutely lost for words. I couldn't say a thing. I just couldn't believe it. He was the last person I expected to die. I mean, Bowie lives a far more reckless life than Bolan ever did, and he's going to live to a hundred.

Adrian:
I don't believe he died. It was a part of me that died, as opposed to someone I knew that died.

Eric Hall:
It was on the ten o'clock news as I was driving to my office, I heard . . . Just couldn't believe it.

Chris Welch, *Daily Mail*:
Miss Jones, mother of Bolan's two-year-old son, Rolan, was taken to hospital with a badly broken jaw. . . . She had still not been told of the tragedy.

Jennifer Sharp:
So many people are killed in car accidents every day and all through the year, but it's just a statistic and it doesn't sort of mean that much to you. But when it's someone that you've known, and it's so immediate, there's this dreadful feeling of mortality. . . .

Chris Welch, *Daily Mail*:
On Thursday night the couple went for a late meal at Morton's, the Berkeley Square restaurant. It was on the way home, as they neared Bolan's rambling detached house in Putney, London SW, that the crash came. The Mini, with Bolan (a non-driver) in the passenger seat, left the road as it crossed a hump-backed bridge. It shot through the fence and smashed into a horse chestnut tree.
Seconds later, Gloria's brother, Richard Jones, came over the bridge in another car and found the wreckage.

June Bolan:
With Paul and Denny (he owns Sweeney's, the hairdressing establishment) I immediately went to his mother's. That was my only concern and I thought: My God! If she knows,

she'll freak! His dad's a porter in this block of flats in Putney and I knocked on the door of these flats in complete hysterics. His father opened the door, took one look at me and slammed it in my face. So I banged again, but this time his brother opened the door. He came and put his arms around me; he could see the state I was in so he led me away from the front door and out into the courtyard, level with the kitchen window. His mother opened the window and screamed at Harry: "Don't cuddle her. Kill her!" Something I shall never forget until the day I die. At this point I got completely hysterical and Harry let go of me; presumably he could see how his mother was. Then his aunt came out to try and stop it, because Harry was going to hit me. He's built like a brick shithouse. This guy's enormous and he was going to hit me! So I put my hands in my fur coat pocket and said: "Harry, if you want to hit me, you just do it, because there's nothing I can do about it." Then I turned and just walked back to the car. He came running after me but instead of hitting me, he started thumping the car, stupid idiot! And all the while his mother was screaming obscenities out of the window.

Talking with fans; August 1977.

Chris Welch, *Daily Mail*:
The Rock world has lost one of the best friends it ever had....

Gloria Jones:
I lost my loved one.

Adrian:
He was the most important factor in my life.

Gloria Jones:
He was the only man I ever really loved, or will love.

Jennifer Sharp:
I came and had a drink in the bar, sitting at the place where we had all been sitting; it's only a few hours later and life goes on much as before, and for him there was no tomorrow; this awful feeling of being eliminated and nothing else but a residue of your personality in people's memories.... Let's hope that if there is something somewhere else, he may be happy.

Gloria Jones:
When Marc died everything just closed up.

June Bolan:
He didn't have a fear of dying as such. We used to stay up night after night because he was petrified of going to sleep; he was afraid that if he went to sleep he might never wake up. And he believed it.

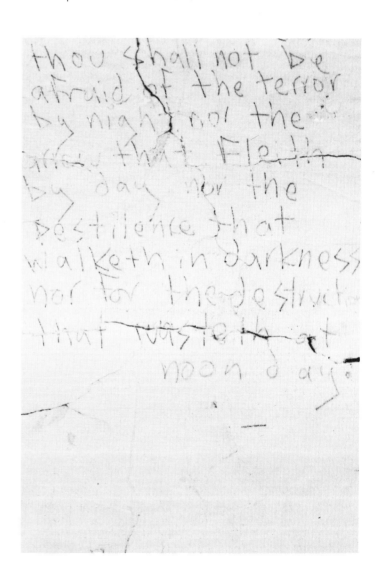

Thou shalt not be afraid
of the terror by night
nor of the arrow that flieth by day
nor of the pestilence that walketh in darkness
nor of the destruction that wasteth at noonday.

... and then, before finally going to sleep, he added:

God's love on the room
Amen.

A prayer which Marc Bolan recited at night before sleeping, a copy of which he carried on his person, wherever he went.

He had such a mind that he could bring things about, so he'd never go to sleep. Sometimes we'd spend three nights up; he used to play Scrabble, backgammon, the guitar, sing songs on the tape; he used to write a lot of poems and I used to read them onto a tape for him. Or if he did happen to go to sleep, he'd make me promise to wake him in half an hour, and I would wake him so he would see he was awake and all right. Then he'd go back for another little sleep.... It wasn't drugs or drink or anything like that. It was just that the big fear in his life was dying in his sleep. I think he was afraid of it happening that way because for him it wasn't a very splendid way to go.... He wasn't afraid of dying. He always believed he'd come back. There was never any doubt about that, never any question.... And that's why, even though he's dead, I still talk about him in the present tense.

Posing for fans outside the T. Rex offices, New Bond Street, July 1977.

Steve Currie:
I've just done the Chris Spedding tour with Tony Newman, who did eighteen months with Marc, and we were talking about him in the present tense.... It's a sad way to go. He was a Rock star, an empty shell. He couldn't do a Peter Noon or an Adam Faith, he couldn't go 'respectable'. It wasn't in his make-up, so maybe he had it coming to him.... He always wanted to be a Rock 'n' Roll star.

June Bolan:
I saw him when he was dead. He was very beautiful. When I uncovered his head I didn't know what I was going to

see but in fact all he had on his face was a tiny scratch, just this little cut on his chin, rather like a sort of deep shaving cut and that was all. I only saw his face and he just looked like he was fast asleep, just very cold when I kissed him.

Tony Visconti:
My wife and I attended Marc's funeral, which was one of the saddest moments of my life.

The Guardian, Sept. 21st 1977:
Admirers of the pop singer Marc Bolan, gathered round a white swan sculpted in flowers at his funeral in London yesterday....
The swan was surrounded by fans at the service in Golders Green, London. Rod Stewart and David Bowie also arrived for the funeral.
The swan, made of chrysanthemums, was 4 ft high and 5 ft long. At its base was the word *Marc* traced in flowers of red, green, blue and silver. It was from the singer's manager and friend, Tony Howard, and a symbol of one of Mr Bolan's biggest hits, RIDE A WHITE SWAN, made by his band, T. Rex, in 1970. It bore the message: "In life, in death, in love."

Tony Visconti:
The funeral was almost like a circus. We were invited by EMI to drive in seven or eight limousines that they had hired; I went in a limousine with David Platz and my wife, Mary (Hopkin) with two other people, and we were really disgusted. There were genuine fans there, who were crying for Marc, but there were lots of other fans there with cameras, and autograph books. As soon as a pop star stepped out of a limousine, you would have a segment of the fans — I'm not saying all — but some of them would come rushing up with autograph books, forgetting that this was a funeral, with his family present.

The *Guardian*:
Other wreaths and bouquets were from Elton John, Cliff Richard, Alvin Stardust, Keith Moon, Gary Glitter and members of T. Rex.

Tony Visconti:
It was a travesty of a funeral and I was bitterly upset. I was sitting up in the balcony of the service and everyone could hear Marc's mother weeping very loudly; she was really crying her heart out, and his brother was crying. June was sitting away from me and she was crying.

June Bolan:
They tried to ban me from the funeral; they wouldn't tell me where the body was, so I got Scotland Yard to take me. I went to the funeral, but I kept a very low profile.

The Guardian:
Among the mourners were Alvin Stardust, Steve Harley, Mary Hopkin, Linda Lewis and members of the groups, The Damned and Brotherhood of Man.

Tony Visconti:
Cremation is the worst thing! I mean, the automation killed me, the way in which this thing—this arm, like out of Star Wars, just popped up out of the floor and just took the coffin away into the next room. I just couldn't stop crying and I went outside. Mary and I were in a daze. We were looking for our limousine and we got in the wrong one. We were kicked out of that and were just standing there, frozen with shock, when these kids started coming up to Mary and to Rod Stewart, and other people, asking for their autographs.

Thomson Prentice, *Daily Mail*, Sept. 21st 1977:
Pop idols Rod Stewart and David Bowie went almost unnoticed in a mass of mourning fans yesterday. The fans were thinking only of singer Marc Bolan....

Eric Hall:
I remember Mike Mansfield (TV Director) saying to me, when we were sitting in the synagogue, the day of Marc's cremation: "You can almost see him there, dancing about the stage, saying, 'you bloody fools'." There was Bowie, Rod Stewart, Steve Harley, the whole lot. He would have loved that. That's the only way he should have gone.

Thomson Prentice, *Daily Mail*:
Girls in Bolan scarves, hats and badges sobbed hysterically and reached to touch his coffin as it was carried into Golders Green crematorium in North London.

Tony Visconti:
I felt I wanted to get violent with one or two of them; they were making a mockery of this whole thing.

Steve Currie:
It could have been that Marc would have liked his funeral better managed. He would have liked the whole of EMI

square blocked off and all the cars leaving in one long procession.

Thomson Prentice, *Daily Mail*:
There was loud sobbing from his family and friends as Rabbi Henry Goldstein said: "It is ironic that there may have been two Marc Bolans. The real one—a good-natured boy who loved his parents—and the image projected on stage. Now those who knew him as one or other are united to mourn his death."

Tony Visconti:
A ginger-headed kid came over to me and he put his hand out. He said: "Are you Tony Visconti?" I said I was; I was very uptight in case he was going to ask me for my autograph. Well, he said: "I would just like to thank you personally, for helping Marc make such good music over the years." I said: "You're very, very welcome."

June Bolan:
The next day, first thing in the morning, I went and I said: "I want to see the ashes." They said that I couldn't; they said that the only one who could see them was Harry (Marc's brother). "Well, I'm his widow," I said. I was still married to him when he died; we weren't exactly divorced. The man didn't know what to do, I mean, he was just doing his job I suppose. He then went away to consult with someone else and after a few moments he came back and said that he was sorry, but this just wasn't done. I told him I wasn't leaving, so I and a very good friend of mine, Susie Dion, we just sat there. Eventually, he said: "All right then. Come this way." It was beautiful. I had my flowers with me because I couldn't leave them at the funeral; I would have had to have gone with all the other people and his mother would have seen them; I just wouldn't do it. They were gardenias. Nobody knew that Marc's favourite flowers were gardenias. We searched the whole of London for them. At the place where he was cremated they put the urn on the altar and just stood there. I said: "Look, it's all right. I'm not going to steal them. I'm not going to do anything. I just want to talk to him." And that's what I did. I left my little bunch of gardenias and I just talked to him for a while. And then I left. I felt so good; I think, had I not seen him dead, I'd say he wasn't dead. I don't know, he just doesn't seem it. I don't mean he's going to manifest himself or anything like that. He just doesn't seem dead to me.

Gloria Jones:
After the baby was born, Marc wasn't into so much of always trying to live up to being an occult figure, because he was a father. Sure, Marc believed in reincarnation, like anyone else can.

Marc Bolan, as told to Jan Iles, *Record Mirror*, Feb. 1st 1975:
I do believe in reincarnation; I've been back about three times that I know of. I mean, I get these flashes and things. I was a minstrel and that would probably explain why I'm interested in literature, poems and music. I can

remember being a cavalier as well, you know. I remember this place in France that I've visited; it was a sixteenth-century house which I'd never seen before and yet I remember having been there before.

Eric Hall:
I miss him. Of course I miss him. He was a mate, a very close mate.

Steve Harley:
It was the first real feeling of loss I've ever had in my life. I'd never lost anyone that close to me before.

... David is a most sensitive and caring friend....

B. P. Fallon, Jeff Dexter, Marc, Johnny Fingers and Bob Geldorf of The Boomtown Rats; taken during the filming of MARC in Manchester.

B. P. Fallon:
I miss him selfishly, because I can't phone him up; I used to get loony phone calls at five in the morning, you know.

Steve Harley:
He lived as a star; he couldn't live any other way. He believed all his life that he was a legend. He had a massive, but massive ego and it was this that was so endearing about him.

David Wigg, *Daily Express,* **Sept. 29th 1977:**
Rock star, David Bowie, has set up a trust fund for the 'love child' of his late friend Marc Bolan. Two-year-old Rolan Bolan is Marc's son by his common law wife, coloured American singer, Gloria Jones.

Gloria Jones:
The main thing is that Rolan will grow up to know that his father was a wonderful man. I intend to bring Rolan up in the way I feel Marc would have loved.

David Wigg, *Daily Express:*
Bowie set up the trust fund immediately after Marc's funeral. Rolan will come into benefit at the age of 18....

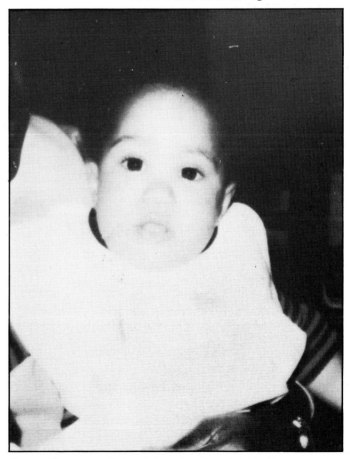
Rolan Seymour Feld Bolan, born to Gloria Jones and Marc, September 26th 1975.

Gloria Jones:
All the time during my pregnancy I never felt I wasn't wanted or the baby wasn't wanted. Marc would take me everywhere with him; I would travel with him and he would work out his schedules — when I got into my later months — to be in London, because he wanted the baby to be born in London. And when I had the baby, Marc was there. He actually helped deliver Rolan with the doctor.

David Wigg, *Daily Express*:
Rolan was not forgotten by Marc. He had settled a trust fund which takes care of him immediately.

Gloria Jones:
He was so sweet to Rolan; he and Rolan, they loved each other. What's so beautiful is, the older Rolan gets the more he's like him; it's Marc walking around looking at me.

David Wigg, *Daily Express*:
Bowie and Marc were close friends. Bowie flew from Switzerland for the funeral and appeared on Marc's last TV show.
Marc was divorced from artist wife June last year. The decree nisi was not absolute until this month. Although his will, made in 1973, has not been published, it is understood he has made a number of bequests. When June Bolan heard of the Bowie trust fund, she said: "It's a wonderful gesture. But then David is a most sensitive and caring friend."

> Every dawn of our lives a heart is forged
> And linked with lore to one so similar
> Born with blessed life dust
> Stored beneath its soul
> To bless and pass onto its children.
> Even though the wind may blow it all away
> Don't ever worry 'cos I'm your friend.
> From A DAY LAYE by Marc Bolan

Fooling around with his hair, pretending to a group of fans, it was a wig.

Adrian:
I was really in love with him; to like Marc is to love Marc.

Eric Hall:
Everybody who ever met him, loved him.

B. P. Fallon:
Primarily what we were, we were two cats who were mates; I mean, we were pals ahead of a working relationship; we were buddies, you know. We used to have fun together, plotting how to conquer the world. Interviews, photo sessions and stuff like that was a game. He saw it as a game, which it is. The whole music business is a game.

Steve Currie:
He was very good to me. I'll defend him to my death. He was a good bloke; always treated me fairly; never any bullshit.

Mickey Finn:
He was a real friend and very inspiring. He meant a lot to me. Marc and I used to be very, very close. We had a soft spot for each other. The bond was that we both liked Rock 'n' Roll so much.

Gloria Jones:
All I know is that the years that we were together, he was a very special man to me and my child. He took care of us and we never had to worry about anything.

Keith Deves, *The Sun*, Dec. 19th 1977:
The love agony of tragic pop superstar Marc Bolan is revealed in his will.

The 30-year-old rock singer has left £10,000 each to his mistress and ex-wife.

Gloria Jones:
I had not known Marc even personally when I was put in his will. Marc put me in his will in '73. I didn't meet him until '72. We weren't having a love affair until the end of the '73, so you see he put me in his will when we were only friends.

Keith Deves, *The Sun*:
A friend said of the identical amounts last night: "Perhaps Marc was just being fair to the end in giving both girls the same."
The will was made in 1973 — the year he began his relationship with the coloured singer.
He left £85,000 in bequests to relatives and friends. Any money left over will go to charities. His parents, Mr and Mrs Feld, are left £20,000. Other people left money in the will — still to be granted probate — include his manager, Tony Howard. He is left £10,000, the same as T. Rex drummer, Mickey Finn.
Record producer, Tony Visconti, husband of Welsh pop singer, Mary Hopkin, is left £5,000.
Marc also remembered the parents of his former wife, Mr and Mrs Anthony Child. They are left £5,000.
The will was made out as "Mark Feld, otherwise known as Marc Bolan" of 47 Bilton Towers, West London.

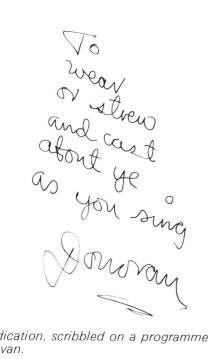

A dedication, scribbled on a programme, to Marc from Donovan.

Tony Visconti:
Marc was extremely tight with his money; very, very tight. In fact, I never expected to be mentioned in his will. We parted company so many years ago, but I was absolutely chuffed, you know. There was five thousand quid just sitting there.

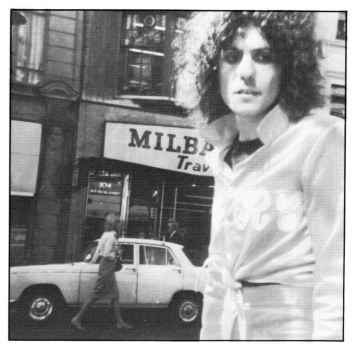

Possibly the last photograph taken of Marc, snapped by a fan two days before his death.

Frank Thompson, *Daily Mail*:
Marc Bolan's girl may face death car charge....

Gloria Jones:
He wanted to marry me. He had always said he wanted to marry me. When I returned to London, just before the accident, he was telling me that we would probably be getting married around January.

June Bolan:
It's very ironic that he had to die in a car crash. He never drove a car in his life, ever. One day he wanted me to teach him to drive. We were out in East Grinstead, Sussex, and there are lots of country roads there, and he suddenly said: "I want you to teach me to drive." I thought, well, all right, it's a Mini, it won't run away with him, fine. So he got in the driver's seat. I put the car in first gear and sat in the passenger's seat. I told him what to do, showed him the clutch, the brake and the accelerator. "You press on the throttle, let the clutch out slowly and the car will go forward," I said. He did all that and without any jerking, the car started to move forward. I suppose we were probably going at about 3 miles an hour, whereupon Marc started shouting: "Stop it. I want to get out, I want to get out!" He didn't know what to do; he felt completely out of control, disconcerted. He never expressed a desire to drive again; never had a licence ... so it's very ironic that he should die in a car crash.

Gloria Jones:
I was trying to finish an album; once the album was completed, then we were going to have another baby.

Frank Thompson, *Daily Mail*:
Marc Bolan's mistress, American singer Gloria Jones, may

face drinking-and-driving charges following the pop star's death in a car crash, it was announced at yesterday's inquest.

Miss Jones ... hobbled into the coroner's court, in Battersea, on crutches, one leg still in plaster two months after the accident.

Inspector William Wilson said that she gave a blood sample after being taken to hospital, seriously injured.

He added: "It has been recommended that Miss Jones be prosecuted for driving while unfit through drink and possibly for driving with excess alcohol in her blood."

Richard Jones recalled yesterday how his sister had mentioned a noise coming from the Mini, and a 'shimmy'.

"I could hear it too," he said. "On the previous day we had had some of the tyres changed and another tyre fitted." That night "there was nothing unusual in the way Gloria was driving," said her brother. He lost sight of her a couple of times and then, as he drove over a hump-backed bridge, he saw that the Mini had crashed. It was "smoking and steaming" and Bolan had been thrown into the back.

In hospital Gloria Jones, her jaw wired up, described what she could of the accident by writing down answers to police questions....

Just before she felt the car pulling to the left and lost all control, "I had a feeling of something having fallen off the car."

Such a loss of control, the inquest was told, could have been caused by the state of the Mini's tyres. Pressure in one at the front which should have been 28 lb per square inch, was only 16 lb. One at the back was also far below the recommended pressure. And two nuts were loose on the nearside front wheel. One took four finger turns to tighten it before a wheelbrace was needed....

After the jury returned a verdict of accident, Gloria Jones and her brother left in a chauffeur-driven Daimler, watched in silence by her dead lover's followers.

They wore badges saying: 'Keep a little Marc in your heart.'

Gloria Jones:
He felt that when he had to leave the country, he felt that maybe he was letting his fans down. This is one thing he always specified; he loved his kids, you know? And he would never leave them. But when you travel quite a bit, you have no control over these things.

Eric Hall:
Sometimes when he was doing a TV series or something, he'd meet a few fans at Euston Station or whatever. He really bothered about them, you know? He'd actually go up to them, hug them, kiss them; he genuinely cared for people. Loved them.

Gloria Jones:
Those kids would do anything in the world for him.

The above photograph of Marc posing with a group of fans, was taken by Mick O'Halloran with Marc's camera and is the property of one of the fans (Steve Finney, extreme right), who tells the following story:
Five fans made their way to Scorpio Studios, where Marc Bolan was involved in a recording session, during August 1975. Vainly, the fans tried to hear the music through the letter box, but after a conversation with Marc, conducted through the same letter box, he invited them in to watch the recording proceedings. During the course of that day, the above photograph was taken, and when the recording session finally ended the following morning, Marc arranged for each of his fans to be driven safely to their homes in a chauffeur-driven car.

Adrian:
We followed him about on the last tour, sleeping in stations, wherever we could. One night we went to the police station and asked them to lock us up for the night, just for somewhere to sleep. The blankets smelt awful. The tour lasted about two weeks in all. Started in Newcastle. He played the best gig ever in Glasgow, March '77. Perfect. The gig was supposed to be on a Saturday but the equipment was held up in Manchester the night before, so they couldn't perform. So Marc played on Sunday and he played his

best. He noticed a friend and myself in the audience and it was just like he was playing to us only. He had that knack. Some of my friends went to France to see him and Marc paid for them to stay in a hotel for the night.

B. P. Fallon:
I meet people around the country and they're Marc people. And there always will be those people.

Steve Harley:
People forget very easily. People are fickle.

Steve Currie:
I was on the Chris Spedding tour. I got a phone call. Some fans of Marc, dressed in black, from various parts of the country. We were playing St Albans the next night, about 150 miles away, and they all travelled by bus to that gig, just to see me, because I was a member of T. Rex. They had a photograph of me and Marc in a silver double case, which they wanted to give to me. For them, it's a life; they don't want to listen to anything nasty said about him, because they believe in Marc as a whole sort of direction of life.

> If tears could build a pathway,
> And memories a lane,
> I'd walk the road to heaven,
> And bring him back again.

A short poem, composed and scribbled on the back of a letter sent to the Editor during the production of this book, by Richard Callahan, a fan from Glasgow.

Adrian:
There was an aura about him.

Gloria Jones:
He walked into a room and you knew that he was some-

Signing autographs outside the T. Rex offices.

body, even if you didn't know who he was.

Adrian:
He always knew what he wanted to do.

Tony Visconti:
He had this Napoleonic complex. Definitely. Maybe some of his fans — a small portion of his fans saw him as God.

Snapped by a fan outside his house in Fulham, London S.W.6.

A photograph of the TV screen during Marc's last performance in his Granada TV series, MARC.

John Peel:
I don't think now that Rock history will remember him as a major figure, but just as a rather interesting minor figure, mainly interesting because I think he was the only person who was able to make the transition from being loved by the 'flower people' to being a Top-of-the-Pops idol.

Steve Harley:
I'm not fickle and I don't forget. I still sit and look at one particular armchair in my living room, where he used to curl up cross-legged all the time.

Gloria Jones:
He was, first of all, a born entertainer.

Bob Hart, *The Sun*, **Jan. 6th 1978:**
Fans salute star Marc....
Pop star Marc Bolan ... has scooped the pool in Britain's top music polls.
Bolan, aged 29, won six awards in the poll, run by the pop paper *Record Mirror*.
Young readers voted Bolan best male vocalist and best-dressed star in 1977.
Marc's TV show, his last album, DANDY, and his band,

T. Rex, were also rated No. 1. And his last British concerts were chosen as best live gigs.
Marc's girlfriend, Gloria Jones, ... was voted best female vocalist in the poll.
Last night a spokesman for *Record Mirror* said: "It seems they have paid him a wonderful final tribute."

Steve Currie:
There'd be no Punks, no Sex Pistols or David Bowie if it wasn't for Marc.

Steve Harley:
He was a brilliant man.

Adrian:
He was just the most beautiful person I ever met; he was just like a little god.

John Peel:
He was like sort of top of the second division. That was his status.

Tony Visconti:
He was a very, very strong person.

Mickey Finn:
He was an outstanding person. His dedication and enthusiasm was incredible.

Steve Currie:
He was the father of seventies Rock 'n' Roll.

Mick O'Halloran:
He just loved life and everything.

June Bolan:
He was a quarter of my life.

Robin Nash:
He was lucky and successful, and he knew exactly how to use it. And he did.

Eric Hall:
He was unique.

Alvin Stardust:
He was a lovely crackpot; you know what I mean, Marc was one of those who had that star thing that you've got to have in show business, and you've got to be a little bit loony.

B. P. Fallon:
He was very important, very magical, very wise, very childish . . . lovely.

Muriel Young:
He was one of the most magical people I have ever known.

Gloria Jones:
He was born to stardom.

Mr Syd Feld:
Marc Bolan's father
He was born to boogie and he danced his way all through life.

My life's a shadowless horse
If I can't get across to you
In the alligator rain
My heart's all pain for you.
From MAMBO SUN by Marc Bolan

... Every dawn of our lives a heart is
forged. . . .

We are the child-ren of Rarn   We've trod-den the vales of the sun   The

In 1970 Marc Bolan began sketching ideas for a major work. Full of mythical references and very much exemplifying his love for imaginary characters, on whom he bestowed mythological sounding names, it was to be entitled THE CHILDREN OF RARN. Sadly, he never completed it.

He did, however, record a selection of the more important themes on tape, just with his own voice accompanied by himself on acoustic guitar, but, for some reason best known to himself, he retreated from developing the project.

Nevertheless, the seeds of something worthwhile were very much there and the potential was more than apparent to a professional ear. Tony Visconti rediscovered his copy of that tape six months after Marc Bolan's death and on hearing it again, was determined to present the tape commercially to the public. With a great deal of skill and sensitive application of modern studio equipment, he has augmented what Marc Bolan initially taped so as to make this proposition possible. (Cube Records, Marc LP HFLD 1.)

The result is beautiful, exciting and underlines Marc Bolan's talent as an artist; it serves, furthermore, as a fitting tribute to his memory.

Here, Tony Visconti tells in his own words, the story of how Marc Bolan came to make that simple, somewhat casual, but certainly significant tape recording in Tony Visconti's flat in Putney, seven years ago. He also describes the techniques he employed in, what Marc himself might well have chosen to describe as, the reincarnation of THE CHILDREN OF RARN.

THE CHILDREN

child will cry, on swans they fly We are the child-ren of Rarn And

We are the children of Rarn
We've trodden the vales of the Sun
The child will cry
On swans they fly
We are the children of Rarn.

And we are the seekers of Space
We've seen our Master's face
It's young and gold
And silvery old
We are the seekers of Space.
        THE CHILDREN OF RARN by Marc Bolan

I really had to search my memory but I came to the conclusion, by looking through my diary, and other methods of
detective work, that it must have been October 1971; Marc
had written it about a year earlier but didn't put it on tape
until that time, in my music room. It was to be my working demo. That's the first time, to my knowledge, that it had
been recorded.

He was very excited. He said it was going to be his Rock
opera. This would be about the time of TOMMY, but it was
in his head long before TOMMY came out; it was going to
be his SERGEANT PEPPER, his monumental work. But we
both realised it was going to involve a lot more work than
just these fifteen or sixteen songs that he had put down.
It would need long instrumental passages, narrative and a
lot of thought would have to go into it. As a result, we
never got around to doing it. In those days we were into
making singles — instant singles and instant albums, which

didn't take very long to make, so we never did get around
to making it properly.

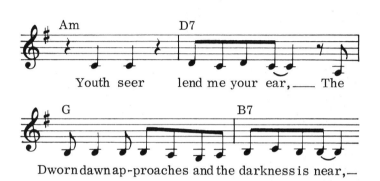

Youth seer   lend me your ear,___ The

Dworn dawn ap-proaches and the darkness is near,—

I was living in this flat of mine at the time. June was
upstairs I remember, with a girlfriend of mine; they were
watching TV and, every now and then, making cups of
tea. Marc and I were sitting downstairs in my music room.
I had a two-track Brenell tape recorder and, as I recall, there
was one table lamp on. It was done in the dark almost; I had
just enough light to see the meters on the machine and I
wore headphones for the whole thing. I wanted to get it all
down faithfully. I took a great deal of trouble even though
it was impromptu and very casual. Mind you, I don't treat
any recording lightly by virtue of my occupation as a
Record Producer. So, I got out my two best microphones
and put one on his voice and one on his guitar. Actually
it was my guitar. It was the only thing available at the
time, my classical guitar with nylon strings on it. He just

I OF RARN

we are the seek-ers of space   We've seen our mas-ter's face   It's

picked it up from the corner of the room and sat down in front of the microphone and did it that way. Had he had his electric guitar, it would have been a different demo.

I don't know much about the story. I do know the imagery is based on the same legends as Tolkien bases his writing on; a time way before recorded history. Marc was a firm

Tree wi-zard___ the

priest is sum-mon-ing,___

Swan king   the

priest is sum-mon-ing,___

Pure tongue   the

priest is sum-mon-ing,___

An-cient one___ the

priest is sum-mon-ing.___

Bap-til-li-ca's Caste, the whip Lord of Dworn,-

Laugh in the wind_ at the sound of the horn, But

fools are young_and their ma-gic is weak_if they

live in the Ta-vern and sleep in the street.___

I monitored it on headphones and he did it almost straight off. I think we stopped the tape recorder in the middle, while he had to refresh his memory. He was quite at ease, quite natural, unlike the environment of a studio, where he'd dress up specially for the session. But in my music room, he was more casual, quite friendly. It was important for him to get the music across to me that day.

believer of the Celtic legends and things like that. I never did get the complete story and possibly he never had the complete story finished; basically, though, it's an obvious black evil force against the good white force, and there are a lot of mythical creatures that Marc invented, like the Dworns and the Lythons; very Tolkien. But the narrative wasn't there; he never did put the narrative down on tape or he might have got John Peel to do it. He was definitely thinking along those lines, of getting someone like Geoffrey Bayldon, the actor who played Cat Weazel on TV; someone to do the narrative in his best middle English voice. What I figured was that Marc had put down a demo and what I would do on top was a demo as well; I'll just sort of sketch what it could have been, rather than do a whole number on it. It wasn't there to begin with. He did a sketch, so consequently I did a sketch. I didn't want to do anything without him. I would have definitely wanted to sit down and discuss those long instrumental passages. I only had a short period of time. When I went to David Platz, there wasn't the time on my side, or the budget available to do it really properly, but then there wasn't enough material to do it properly, in actual fact; certainly not enough of Marc to do two sides and release it as an individual album. There was only about fifteen minutes of music.

young and gold and sil-ver-y old, We are the seek-ers of space. Om!

I was tempted to use Bill Legend, Steve Currie and Mickey Finn, but I only had three days; one day to put the drums down, one day to put the instruments, and one

Bel - tane_ Hu - mane_ You'll_come a -

- gain. Bel - tane____ Hu - mane ___

You'll ___ come a - gain to this

Earth. _____ Repeat ad lib.

to mix the entire thing. So I opted for a professional drummer who could read music, and also a good friend of mine, Andy Duncan. I just sat him down, with the parts in front of him and because of his proficiency, he was able to do it all in a period of four hours; everything — the tom-toms, all the bongo and conga drums, all the tinkly bells. He's a very versatile drummer. I did the bass parts. I did play bass on the earlier T. Rex things, so it wasn't just to save time. There was a temptation to put some lead guitar work on but I thought it would be ultimately unfair. Marc should do that. That's what he was very good at. So I even left out the lead guitar work. I did, maybe, a little riff at the end of WE ARE THE DWORNS. Marc only played two bars of it, so I just played the rest of it out and faded it into his next piece of conversation — next bit of verbal, as he would say. I also played the recorders. Marc loved recorders, and the fact that I used to play them, so I would make an appearance on all the T. Rex records and every album. And keyboards, which I did on THE CHILDREN OF RARN, I played the melotron.

For the strings I used a double string quartet. Any more strings would have been overweight. It would have over-powered Marc's demo, because Marc used to double-track

his voice and he used to triple-track, and quadruple-track his guitars. As I said, I didn't want to put any lead guitar work on the album, so the eight strings balanced out the

July 1976, after a sound check concerning a gig in Wimbledon.

demo very well I think. What I tried to do, I suppose, was to incorporate the whole Tyrannosaurus Rex and T. Rex sound right from the beginning. I wanted to use the early sound and also the latest sounds that Marc used. I'm sure that was what Marc had in his mind, to go very acoustic on some numbers, very soft and gentle, which he was in the very early days; and then to go extremely hard with hundreds of over-dubbed electric guitars on some of the tracks. But I didn't take it to that extreme because of what I had to work with.

There was one little track we did on the WE ARE THE DWORNS tracks. I fed his acoustic guitar through a guitar amplifier and through a fuzz box. I made his guitar very fuzzy and very electric sounding. For a nylon string guitar to sound like that was quite amazing. That was about all I could do with Marc's thing, because his voice was also on the guitar and I didn't want to get too much fuzz on his voice. There was a leakage from the guitar track to the vocal track, but I kept it down to a minimum.

The only argument I had with Marc was that if he wanted to make it really impressive musically, we would really have to do some hard work and hard thinking on the musical level. Change the keys a bit. Marc only knew about seven chords which only enabled him to play in about three keys. THE CHILDREN OF RARN is in only about three keys which is not enough in any symphonic work, or any large work. You need to modulate; you need to have one key going into another strange key to create a mood. Marc was aware of this but didn't know how to achieve it. When I used to orchestrate for him he would only let me go so far; I had to keep the string arrangements simple.

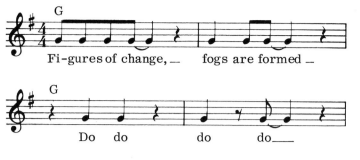

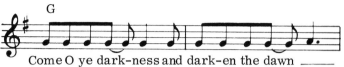

not speaking to him for a year, his roadie phones me up, instead of him personally, and we were such good friends up until that split up. Quite honestly, I didn't bother to look for the tape.

He didn't do anything with THE CHILDREN OF RARN because he was frightened I think. He knew it would take a lot of work and he was putting most of his energy, sad to say, into exploiting the media, rather than the media exploiting him. He was doing his best to get his picture in the papers every week, doing radio interviews, TV shows and all that. He was determined to become the biggest star ever out of Great Britain. He wanted to outshine the Beatles and, again sadly, he neglected the musical side to his career. I mean, he was totally music until he got his first two hit singles, then he became aware of how nice it was to see his picture in the papers every week. So I think he was a little afraid of tackling THE CHILDREN OF RARN, when he'd sit back and have a listen to it. He had a copy of it; I mean, my copy isn't the only one in existence. But he lost his. I remember, after we split, around 1974, he had his roadie phone me up from Los Angeles; this would be about 1975. He said that Marc wanted THE CHILDREN OF RARN tape, but by that time I'd forgotten all about it, that it was recorded even. I told him I was about to move and that all my tapes were in boxes, but if I could find it, I'd send it. Marc had split with June by this time, but I phoned her and asked her if she had a copy. She said that she didn't; in fact, she didn't have any of Marc's possessions any longer. I must admit I wasn't feeling in the greatest or friendliest of attitudes towards Marc at that time; after

But after his death, and because of an incident at the funeral, it became urgent for me to find that tape, to do it and see it through. I really made myself dive into all my tapes and look for that one. And I found it. After hours and hours, covered in dust, I finally found that tape. It was this ginger-headed kid at the funeral, the one who came up to me, put his hand out and just personally thanked me for helping Marc make such good music over the years. For him, and people like him, that's why I had to find that tape, take it to David Platz and do what I did.

Tony Visconti

THE SONGS

BELTANE WALK

Words & Music by MARC BOLAN.

RIFF (walk)

1. Trucking down by the road-side   Met a man with star hide
2. Bopping down by the whirl-pool   I met a girl she was God's tool

He said: "Boy would-n't you like to look?"
I said: "Girl would-n't you like to rock?"

But could it   CHORUS Give me love   gim-me lit-tle love

Gim-me lit-tle love from her heart   Gim-me love   gim-
God's

me lit-tle love from her heart   And then we'll
God's

3. Walking down by the west wind
   I met a boy he was my friend
   I said "Boy we could sing it too" and we do
   Give us love - give us little love
   Give us little love from your hearts
   Give us love - give us little love
   From your hearts
   And then we'll walk

CHILDREN OF THE REVOLUTION

Words & Music by MARC BOLAN.

A DAY LAYE

Words & Music by MARC BOLAN.

DEBORA

Words & Music by MARC BOLAN.

DESDEMONA

Words & Music by MARC BOLAN.

DIAMOND MEADOWS

Words & Music by MARC BOLAN.

GET IT ON

Words & Music by MARC BOLAN.

2. You're built like a car
You've got a hub cap diamond star halo
You're built like a car oh yeah
You're an untamed youth that's the truth
with your cloak full of eagles
You're dirty sweet and you're my girl.

3. You're windy and wild
You've got the blues in your shoes and your stockings
You're windy and wild oh yeah
You're built like a car
You've got a hub cap diamond star halo
You're dirty sweet and you're my girl.

4. You're dirty and sweet clad in black don't look back
and I love you.
You're dirty and sweet oh yeah
You dance when you walk so let's dance take a chance
understand me
You're dirty sweet and you're my girl.

(Chorus Fade)

HOT LOVE

Words & Music by MARC BOLAN.

36 bars per minute

Well she's my wo-man of gold — and she's not — ve-ry old — A- a- ha —
(ain't) no — witch — and I love — the way she twitch A- a- ha —
(fast) - er than most — and she lives — on — the coast A- a- ha —
(ain't) no — witch — and I love — the way she twitch A- a- ha —

Well she's my wo-man of gold — and she's not
Well she ain't — no — witch — and I love —
Well she's fast — er than most — and she lives —
Well she ain't — no — witch — and I love —

I LOVE TO BOOGIE

Words & Music by MARC BOLAN.

2. Well you'd better sneak out with your tail feathers high
    Jitterbug left us vowing to the sky
    With your black velvet cape and your stow pipe hat
    Bebop baby the dance is where it's at
    I love to boogie
    Yes I love to boogie on a Saturday night.
    (Fade on Chorus)

JEEPSTER

Words & Music by MARC BOLAN.

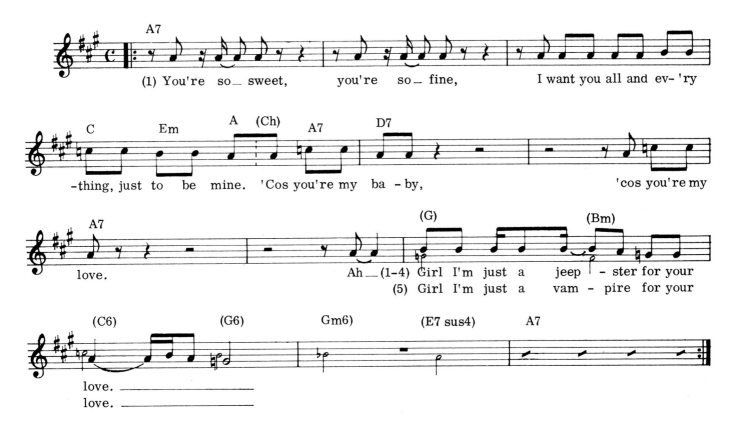

(1) You're so sweet, you're so fine, I want you all and ev-'ry -thing, just to be mine. 'Cos you're my ba-by, 'cos you're my love.

Ah — (1-4) Girl I'm just a jeep - ster for your love.

(5) Girl I'm just a vam - pire for your love.

(2) You slide so good with bones so fair,
You've got the universe reclining in your hair 'cos etc.

(3) Just like a car you're pleasing to hold,
I'll call you Jaguar if I may be so bold 'cos etc.

(4) The wild winds blow upon your frozen cheeks,
The way you flip your hip it always makes me weak 'cos etc.

(5) Your motivation is so sweet,
Your vibrations are burning up my feet 'cos etc.

METAL GURU

Words & Music by MARC BOLAN.

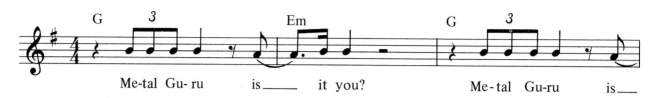

Me-tal Gu-ru is ___ it you? Me-tal Gu-ru is ___

___ it you? Sit-tin' there ___ in your own big chair oh

yeh Me-tal Gu-ru is ___ it true? Me-tal Gu-ru is ___

___ it true? All a-lone ___ with-out a te-le-phone ___ oh yeh. ___

___ Me-tal Gu-ru could ___ it be? You're gon-na bring my

ba-by to me she'll ___ be wild you know a rock and roll child oh yeh. ___

Me-tal Gu-ru how's it been? Just like a sil-ver speed

sa-bre tooth dream.___ I'll be cling-ing on the hitch-ing ma-chine oh yeh.

Me-tal Gu-ru is ___ it you? Me-tal Gu-ru is ___

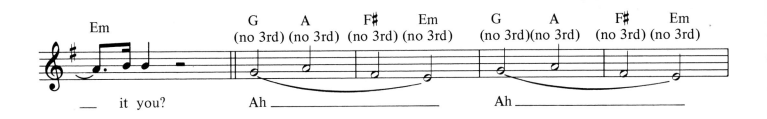

___ it you? Ah _____ Ah _____

Me-tal Gu-ru could ___ it mean

you're gon-na bring my ba-by to me? She'll be wild___ you know a

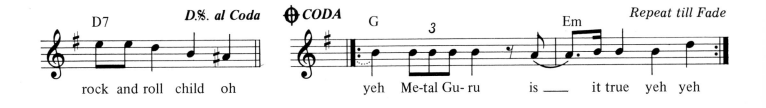

rock and roll child oh yeh Me-tal Gu-ru is ___ it true yeh yeh

NEW YORK CITY

Words & Music by MARC BOLAN.

RIFF

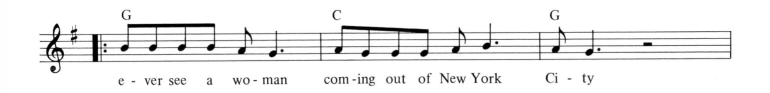

Did you

e - ver see a wo - man com - ing out of New York Ci - ty

with a frog in her hand.___ Well did you

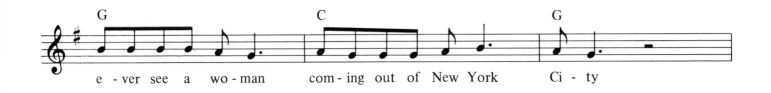

e - ver see a wo - man com - ing out of New York Ci - ty

with a frog in her hand.___

I've been___ don't you know _____ I've been___ don't you

RIDE A WHITE SWAN

Words & Music by MARC BOLAN.

TELEGRAM SAM

Words & Music by MARC BOLAN.

VERSE

1. Te - le-gram Sam_ Te - le-gram Sam_ you _____ I'm_

__ her main man. __ Gold - en note Slim_ gold -

en note Slim_ I _____ knows_ where you've been, ____ yo.

Pur - ple pie Pete_ pur - ple pie Pete_ your

lips that I like it goes munch_ in the heat yeh.

CHORUS

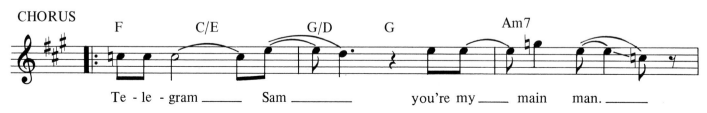

Te - le - gram ____ Sam ____ you're my ___ main man. ____

Te - le - gram _____ Sam _____ you're my _____ main man. _____

2. Bob -

VERSE

- by's al - right _____ Bob - by's al - right _____ he's a

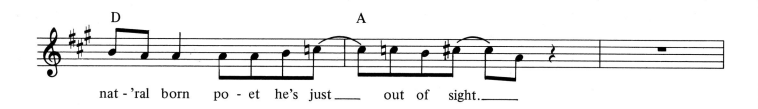

nat - 'ral born po - et he's just _____ out of sight. _____

Jun - gle faced Jake _____ jun - gle faced Jake I say make _____

_____ no mis -take a- bout jun -gle faced Jake Jake.

3. Bobby's alright Bobby's alright
    He's a natural born poet he's just out of sight.
    Automatic shoes automatic shoes
    Give me 3 D vision and the California blues.
    Me out of funk but I don't care
    I ain't no square with my corkscrew hair.

20TH CENTURY BOY

Words & Music by MARC BOLAN.

Men say it's fine men __ say it's good ev -

- 'ry - bo - dy say it's just __ like rock __ and roll. __

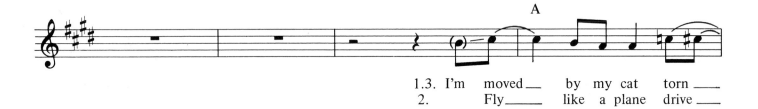

1.3. I'm moved __ by my cat torn __
2. Fly __ like a plane drive __

__ by my ram sting __ by my bee }
__ like a car hold by the hand } Babe __ I wan-na be your man..

__ Well it's plain __

DISCOGRAPHY

1965–1969

1965	The Wizard	Mark Bowland	Decca
1966	The Third Degree	Mark Bolan	Decca
1967	Hippy Gumbo	Mark Bolan	Columbia
1967	Desdemona	Johns Children	Track
1968	Deborah – Tyrannosaurus Rex		Regal Zonophone
1968	My People were Fair and Had Sky in their Hair (L.P.)	Tyn. Rex	R.Z.
1968	One Inch Rock	Tyn. Rex	R.Z.
1969	Pewter Suitor	Tyn. Rex	R.Z.
1969	Unicorn (L.P.)	Tyn. Rex	R.Z.
1969	King of the Rumbling Spires	Tyn. Rex	R.Z.

1970–1971 Hits

1970	By the Light of the Magical Moon (with Mickey)	Tyn. Rex	R.Z.
1970	A Beard of Stars (L.P.)	Tyn. Rex	R.Z.

As T. Rex

1970	Ride a White Swan	,,	Fly
1971	Hot Love	,,	Fly
1971	Get It On	,,	Fly
1971	Jeepster	,,	Fly

L.P's

1971	T. Rex	,,	Fly
1971	Electric Warrior	,,	Fly

1972 Hits

1972	Telegram Sam	,,	T. Rex
1972	Debora	,,	Magni Fly
1972	Metal Guru	,,	T. Rex
1972	Children of the Revolution	,,	T. Rex
1972	Solid Gold Easy Action	,,	EMI Marc

DISCOGRAPHY

L.P.'s

1972	Bolan Boogie	,,	Fly
1972	The Slider	,,	EMI
1972	Doubleback (double L.P.)	Tyn. Rex	Fly

1973 Hits

1973	Twentieth Century Boy	T. Rex	EMI Marc
1973	Tanx (L.P.)	T. Rex	EMI
1973	The Groover	T. Rex	EMI
1973	Truck on Tyke	T. Rex	EMI

1974 Hits

1974	Teenage Dream	Marc Bolan	EMI Marc
1974	Zinc Alloy & the Hidden Riders of Tomorrow or A Creamed Cage in August (L.P.)		EMI
1974	Marc Bolan — The Beginning of Doves		Track
1974	Light of Love		EMI
1974	Zip Gun Boogie		EMI

1975 Discs

1975	New York City		EMI
1975	Dreamy Lady		EMI

1976 Discs

1976	London Boys		EMI
1976	I Love To Boogie		EMI
1976	Laser Love		EMI
1976	Futuristic Dragon		EMI

1977 Discs

1977	Hot Love—re-issue		Cube
1977	To Know Him is to Love Him	(with Gloria)	EMI
1977	Soul of My Suit		EMI
1977	Dandy in the Underworld		EMI
1977	Bolan's Best + 1		Cube
1977	Celebrate Summer		EMI

1978 Discs

1978	Hot Love E.P.		Cube
1978	Crimson Moon		EMI
1978	Marc: Words and Music		Cube

Living is driving me
hard, I'm just giving
the scat off my pants
for some rich boy
afraid to call me
freind & smile

hendrix, I love the way
dylan his guitar xploded
head ~~boy~~ the way ~~my~~ his
~~told~~ it
Made me understand
Me-e

ageing, ~~Makes~~ you ~~~~
cage & I'm
rageing - is time the
anaimal on
me

Original manuscript illustrating Marc's unusual handwriting and a possible tendency towards dislexia.

... If I can't get across to you ... my heart's
all pain for you.